Options

FOR
EQUITY
INVESTORS

Options

FOR
EQUITY
INVESTORS

Increasing Sharemarket Returns using
Exchange Traded Equity Options

Wendy Newton

Wrightbooks

First published 2002 by Wrightbooks
an imprint of John Wiley & Sons Australia, Ltd
33 Park Road, Milton, Qld 4064

Offices also in Sydney and Melbourne

Typeset in 11/13.2pt Jouillard

National Library of Australia
Cataloguing-in-Publication data

Newton, Wendy Lynn
Options for equity investors: increasing sharemarket returns using
exchange traded equity options.

Includes index.
ISBN 0 701637 19 6.
1. Stock options - Australia. 2. Options (Finance) - Australia.
3. Investments - Australia. I. Title.

332.63280994

Cover design by Rob Cowpe

Printed in Australia by McPherson's Printing Group

10 9 8 7 6 5 4 3 2 1

Disclaimer

The material in this publication is of the nature of general comment only, and
neither purports nor intends to be advice. Readers should not act on the basis
of any matter in this publication without considering (and if appropriate, taking)
professional advice with due regard to their own particular circumstances. The
author and publisher expressly disclaim all and any liability to any person, whether
a purchaser of this publication or not, in respect of anything and of the
consequences of anything done or omitted to be done by any such person in
reliance, whether whole or partial, upon the whole or any part of the contents
of this publication.

CONTENTS

FOREWORD

The rapid growth in global options markets over the 1990s has provided professional and retail investors with unprecedented trading opportunities, combined with the unique ability to protect their investments against unexpected market falls.

At a time where more and more of us are turning to equity markets as the primary source of income for self-funded retirement, an ability to trade the options market has never been more important. Not only can this book teach you how to increase your income, but perhaps more importantly, it will help you to gain the knowledge, skills and confidence to acquire and then protect your equity investments.

The careful use of options has been a standard part of professional money managers' strategies for many years. Through Wendy's book you will learn an 'insider's' perspective to the market and be taught how to compete successfully for profits with the professionals. Her years of experience as a trader, retail futures and options adviser, and then strategist and educator for the Australian Stock Exchange (ASX) have given her a unique ability to understand the core motivations and psychology of the market and its participants.

In her role as National Manager—Market Development, Wendy was instrumental in the development and implementation of the acclaimed Derivatives Adviser Accreditation Policy for the ASX, and oversaw the education of more than 10,000 private investors and brokers. Through this book you can take the benefit of not only her experiences, but also of many leading traders and advisers with whom she has developed lasting relationships.

Against this background, Wendy's book provides a step-by-step approach to understanding options theory, and a solid, practical approach to the implementation and execution of trading strategies no matter how simple or complex their nature.

Frank Dunphy
Managing Director
Bendigo Stock Exchange

1 THE VERSATILITY OF OPTIONS

Chapter objectives:

- Emphasise that options are an alternative to outright share ownership and can be used to complement your share trading
- Distinguish between exchange traded options and company options
- Introduce the concepts of call and put options
- Describe five basic ways you can use options within your share trading
- Discuss ways of using this book.

As a share investor, you know all about buying shares. You check the share prices daily, take an active interest in where the overall market is, you read the financial press to understand the machinations of the companies in which you're interested in investing. You know how to check for shares that provide the best capital growth and for those that deliver a good yield. You probably use fundamental factors like PE ratios to work out whether the shares are under- or over-valued. You might even use some technical indicators like moving averages to give yourself that extra edge in timing your buying. In short, you're careful about what goes into your portfolio. But then what?

Like most share investors, you know how to buy when the market is rising. That's the easy bit. However, sharemarkets move in three directions: up, down and sideways. What do you do when the market is falling? Do you fall with it? Do you tell yourself you're not really 'losing' since you still own the shares? Do you panic-sell? What about when the share price has stalled? Do you wait in frustration on the sidelines until it starts moving again?

Riding out small declines and flat periods in the sharemarket is a normal part of holding a long-term investment. Nevertheless, there are times when it's smarter to use the market movement, or lack of it, to your advantage. Improving the returns on your existing shareholding should be as natural a part of your investment strategy as carefully adding new holdings to it. So what can you use to give an extra boost to your shares' performance?

Equity options are one of the most flexible tools for trading the sharemarket and improving the returns on your portfolio. They allow you to tailor your market view for bullish, bearish and neutral moves, as well as set the amount of risk you wish to adopt for a particular move, share or sector. Options allow you to increase your exposure to a particular company or decrease it, reduce the risk of a particular holding or eliminate it altogether. They allow you to gain extra income, diversify your portfolio, and to profit from price moves without even having any share ownership—and all for a fraction of the cost of investing in the shares themselves. So just as the name suggests, options give you an investment choice, offering an alternative and a complement to your outright share trading.

So what's the catch, I hear you say? It can't be that easy or everyone would be doing it, right? I mean, you've heard that the professionals use options, that's how the fund managers get their extra returns, that's why you invest your money with them. They can do it, but can you? I guess the best answer is to point out that the majority of equity options traded on the Australian Stock Exchange (the Exchange) are traded by retail investors—not by the professionals, but by people like you and me. So, if you're not already using options to improve your share trading, you're being left behind. And now that you know that, it's time to get with it, and learn how you can improve your sharemarket returns using exchange traded equity options.

Exchange Traded Equity Options versus Company Equity Options

Before we jump into what options are and how you can use them within an equity portfolio, it's really important to distinguish between the two types of equity options: exchange traded and company options.

Company equity options are options issued by a company over its own shares. For example, the company COD Pty Ltd might decide to issue COD options. COD Pty Ltd would then make decisions on things such as how many COD options are issued, what their issue (or exercise) price is, when the expiry date is, etc. If you were to decide to take up the right underlying the option (that is, you choose to exercise your option to take up the COD shares), it would result in an increased issued share capital for that company.

Exchange traded equity options are options listed by the Exchange. Say, for example, ABC shares are already listed on the Exchange, and the Exchange decides to list ABC options over those shares. The Exchange then decides on what their issue, or 'exercise', prices will be, when the expiry date is, etc. These are options over existing shares, and their exercise does not increase the issued share capital for ABC. ABC Pty Ltd not only has no say in whether the options are listed, but is not a party to the traded options. If you trade exchange traded options, you deal directly with the Exchange via your broker. In addition, exchange traded options are created when investors buy and sell them—in other words, the option is created when a buyer and seller agree on a price at which to trade. This means that there is no set number listed by the Exchange. Table 1.1, below, summarises the differences between exchange traded and company options.

Table 1.1
Exchange Traded Equity Options versus Company Equity Options

Exchange Traded Equity Option	Company Equity Option
Listed by the Exchange	Issued by the company
Traded on the Exchange on a separate options market	Traded on the Exchange and on the same market as shares
Company is not a party to transaction	Company is a party to transaction
No set number listed—created between investors	Set number issued by company
Dealings over existing shares— exercise does not increase issued share capital	Exercise does increase issued share capital

We're going to deal exclusively with exchange traded options in this book, so if you want more information on how to trade company options, you'll need to speak with your broker.

What are exchange traded options, and why buy and sell them?

The Basics of Options

Simply stated, an option gives you exposure to a particular share's price movement over a limited period of time. Options provide you with an alternative to buying or selling shares outright and give you time to decide if you want to buy or sell the underlying shares.

There are two types of options. Essentially, a **call option** gives the purchaser the right to buy shares, and a **put option** gives the purchaser the right to sell shares.

You'll learn the details about calls and puts and how you can use them as you work through the book, but in the meantime, let's look at some general ways you can use options.

Participate in Shares You Don't Own

As a share investor you probably enjoy the concept that you 'own' a part of a company. It feels solid and substantial. However, with so many companies listed on the Exchange, unless you have unlimited wealth it is virtually impossible to own a part of all the best performers. You have to decide which of the shares will be the very best, which you'll add to your portfolio. And there's nothing more frustrating than finding that the particular shares you selected have failed to perform as well as the rest of the market or sector.

A call option gives the purchaser exposure to the underlying shares for a limited period of time. This means you have the opportunity of taking advantage of price movements in shares that you're not holding in your portfolio, as well as time to decide if you want to add the physical shares to it. Even if you decide you don't want to buy the shares, you can still make a profit from the underlying share price movement by trading the call option alone.

Diversify Your Portfolio

No doubt you know that one of the golden rules of share investing is to diversify your portfolio, but you may not have the necessary funds to buy exposure across a wide enough range of shares. The costs of call options are a fraction of those of purchasing the shares, so they allow you to gain exposure to a much wider range of shares than you thought you could afford.

Earn Extra Income

When your shares go up you're probably happy and when they go down you're probably unhappy, frustrated, nervous, etc. But how do you feel when they stay fairly flat? Do you view this as a natural part of holding a portfolio of shares, and think, 'At least I'm not losing anything'?

Just as there are times when your shares trend up or down, there are periods, sometimes lengthy, when they stay within a fairly narrow range. By selling or writing call options during flat markets, you can take advantage of the lack of movement. Writers of call options earn income, almost like extra dividends during quiet times, which can improve the returns on their portfolios.

Protect Your Share Portfolio

If you're a long-term share investor, you're probably used to riding out small declines in the sharemarket. However, what if you believe there will be an unusually large decline in a particular share price? Obviously you can sell your shares, but what if you get it wrong and the price rises instead? What can you do to protect the value of your shareholding without selling your shares prematurely? Wouldn't it be nice if you could sell your shareholding only if the share price falls, but at today's higher price?

A put option gives the purchaser the right but not the obligation to sell a parcel of underlying shares (usually 1,000) at a set price. The key words here are 'not the obligation'—in other words, you can wait and see what the share price does before deciding whether to sell or hold your shares. For a limited period of time you can lower the company or specific risk of holding your shares in a falling market, and in addition have time to decide if you still want to sell or continue holding the shares in your portfolio. And if you decide to sell, you've already locked in a higher selling price than that of the current market.

Switch Exposure from an Underperforming Stock to a Better-Performing One

There may be times when a favourite stock in your portfolio is failing to perform, but you see another stock that you feel will perform well over this period. You have a dilemma—you don't really want to sell your favourite shares and incur the high transaction costs of buying them back at a later time. But what can you do to offset this short-term lack of performance, and capitalise on your view of the other stock?

By buying a put option over your existing shares, and simultaneously buying a call option over the new shares, you effectively switch exposure from one stock to the other, without ever having to transact in the physical sharemarket. Not only do you avoid high transaction costs, but you have time to see whether or not you still want to hold your existing shares.

Buy Shares Lower than the Rest of the Market

There may be occasions when you want to buy shares but think they are overpriced. Furthermore, you expect that once the market realises they are overpriced, there will be a small decline in price. Your plan is to wait for that short-term correction and buy the shares once they have dipped. But what if you could earn some extra income during this small decline? Wouldn't you like to be able to buy the shares at an even cheaper price?

Put option writers earn income during quiet markets, which helps to offset the purchasing price of their shares. This means they have the opportunity of buying shares at a 'discount', due to the receipt of the premium.

Using this Book

You can see how versatile options are within a share portfolio, allowing you to tailor your sharemarket strategy to specifically fit your market view. Even more than that, options are an ideal way of setting the exact amount of risk that you wish to adopt within your share portfolio—they can be used to reduce or increase risk or even eliminate it altogether. Want to know exactly how you can do all these things? Then stay with me, and we'll move onto the definitions, concepts and specific strategies that will help you enhance your sharemarket returns.

In order to get the most out of this book, I've designed it to allow you to move through the text in either a linear fashion, that is, from cover to cover, or to move between the chapters based on references within the text. It all depends on your level of current knowledge and the way you find it easiest to learn. So feel free to jump to later chapters if it makes sense for you to do so. In addition, the main chapter points are highlighted by the exclamation icons. If you want to skip a chapter, you might just want to read these before moving forward. Alternatively, they provide a useful way of revising the text later on. The rest is up to you. Enjoy!

2 BASIC PRINCIPLES AND JARGON

Chapter objectives:

- Provide a generic definition of an option
- Demonstrate how a generic call option works in the 'real world'
- Introduce the concepts of novation and standardisation of exchange traded options
- Describe the components of an option.

You've probably already heard that options are complicated instruments and there's a lot of jargon relating to them. Well, I'd like to tell you something different, but unfortunately the jargon part is right. Think of it as learning a brand new language, a language that you need to learn to travel to an exotic destination you've always wanted to visit.

Definition of an Option

By pure textbook definition:

 An option is a contract between two parties which gives the buyer (taker) the right, but no obligation, to buy or sell an underlying security at a specified price, within a specified time, and for an agreed premium.

Personally, I think that's one of the worst definitions I've ever read. Let's break that down into its components so you get a better understanding of what it is:

- It's a contract, therefore it's a legally binding agreement.
- It's between two parties, so for every option there must be a buyer and a seller.
- It gives the buyer, who is more generally referred to as the taker, the right but no obligation.
- The right is to buy in the case of a call, or to sell in the case of a put.
- There's an underlying security, which in the case of an equity option is a parcel of shares.
- There's a specified price at which the taker can buy or sell.
- There's a specified time that the option exists.
- There's an agreed premium, or cost, to the option, paid by the taker and given to the seller (who is more generally referred to as the writer).

Let's look at how an option might work in the real world.

A Simple Example

Let's say you have a neighbour who has two 1,000 hectare blocks of land for sale, each selling for $40,000. One block is at the side of your house and the other backs onto your property, and you decide that if you purchase one block you can build that extension or pool you've always wanted. Either block would suit your needs, but there's one problem. Your money is tied up in a fixed-interest term deposit for the next three months, and if you take it out early the bank will charge you an interest penalty. You really want to buy the land, but don't want to forgo the interest if you can help it. On the other hand, if you wait until your money is free both blocks may be sold.

So you speak with your neighbour and explain the situation, and he agrees to hold one block for you for the next three months, in exchange for you paying him $1,000. The only catch is, he's not going to give you the $1,000 back if you change your mind and decide not to buy it. You do your calculations and decide that this is cheaper than making an early withdrawal, so you agree to it. You pay him the $1,000 and the deal is done. You now have the right to buy your neighbour's 1,000 hectares of land for $40,000 for the next three months, after which the right expires. And for having this right, you have paid him $1,000.

The deal you have struck with your neighbour has all the components of a call option. In other words, there is:

- a right, but no obligation, for you to buy
- an underlying security of 1,000 hectares of land
- a specified price of $40,000
- a specified time of three months
- an agreed premium of $1,000, paid whether you take up your right or not.

Not only have you bought yourself the right to buy the land, you've also bought yourself time to decide if this is a good choice. In other words, over the next three months you can decide whether you still want to buy it, depending on what the market price of the land does over that time. You can get a good feel for this by seeing what happens to the price of the other block over the next three months. There are only three things it could do: it could go up, it could go down, or it could go sideways. So how do these three different market conditions impact on your decision? The next three points show the outcome of our three market conditions:

1. The price rises

Let's say your neighbour has had a lot of buying interest in the land and he decides to increase the price to $45,000. Remember, you have the right to buy your block for $40,000. Would you exercise your right? Probably yes, because by purchasing it through exercise, your total cost of $41,000 (remember, you already paid $1,000 premium) would be less than its current market value. You have a profit already built into your block.

2. The price falls

Alternatively, there may be little buying interest in the land, and in this case your neighbour is forced to reduce the price to $35,000. Would you exercise your option? Probably not, because there would be no point in paying $40,000 for your block through exercise when you could allow your option to expire and purchase the other block for only $35,000.

3. The price stays the same

Finally, what if the price of the other block stays at $40,000—do you exercise your call? If you still want to purchase the block you would, but whether you purchase it through exercise or allow it to expire and purchase the other block, the cost to you would be the same.

So this example shows you two things:

As a buyer of a call option, you have a choice. You have a right but no obligation to buy the underlying asset, and this means you have time to decide if you want to buy it. Whether or not you decide to buy it will depend on what happens to the value of the underlying asset over the life of your option.

In addition, as a buyer of a call option you want the price of the underlying asset to rise over the life of your option. In that way, you have locked in a lower buying price and, at the same time, an inbuilt profit.

Creating an Options Market—Novation

Somewhat like trading shares, when an option buyer and seller agree on the price to be paid for the option, the option is traded. However, if this link between buyer and seller remained throughout the life of the option, you would not be able to exit the option earlier than the expiry date unless the other party agreed to it. Looking back to the land example, what do you think would happen if after two months passed you were to decide you no longer wanted to purchase the land, and therefore no longer wanted the option? Would your neighbour be understanding and offer to pay back some of the premium you paid? More than likely, no.

In order to give you the flexibility of exiting early, the Exchange breaks the link between option buyer and seller and acts as middleman between the two parties. This process is referred to as **novation**. Novation helps create a market which buyers and sellers can freely enter and leave without reference to the original party to the transaction.

Standardisation

If buyers and sellers are entering and exiting the market without reference to each other, how do you know what you're getting when you buy an option? The answer is that the Exchange standardises the components of every option contract, as follows:

1. The underlying security is set at 1,000 shares per one option contract

Be aware that this can change during the life of the option if there is a bonus or rights issue, or some other form of capital reconstruction.

11

If this happens, you need to speak to your broker to see how it might affect your position. For ease of understanding, the references to underlying shares throughout this book will always be 1,000 for every option contract.

> **(!)** With 1,000 shares for every one option, you can see why options are referred to as 'leveraged' or 'geared' instruments. For a small amount of premium (nowhere near the full cost of the underlying shares) you gain exposure to a large number of shares, and your profits and losses are made as if you owned them already.

Leverage gives you the advantage of large exposure for a small initial outlay, but beware—leverage is the proverbial 'two-edged sword', as increased exposure also leads directly to increased risk.

2. *The 'exercise price', or 'strike price', is the specified price of the option. It is the price at which you can buy or sell the underlying shares.*

In the land example, this was set at $40,000. With options, the Exchange sets a range of exercise prices for every option stock listed. In this way, you choose how close you wish to trade to the current share price, and therefore how much premium you're willing to pay.

Currently, the Exchange sets the range of exercise prices at specific intervals according to the value of the stock. The higher the value of the stock, the larger the intervals between the exercise prices. Typically, you will see exercise prices set at intervals of 10¢, 25¢, 50¢ and $1.00, depending on the value of the stock. However, bear in mind that option exercise prices are quoted without decimal points. So, for example, a BHP call option with a $10.00 exercise price will be listed as a BHP 1000 Call.

Be aware that the exercise price may change during the life of the option if there is a bonus or rights issue, or some other form of capital reconstruction. If this happens during the life of your option, you need to speak to your broker to see how it might affect your position.

Generally, if an exercise price does not fit into one of the above categories (for example, you see a BHP 1157 option listed), it indicates that there has been an adjustment to the contract. If you see this sort of price, it is a good idea to check to see if the number of underlying shares has also been adjusted.

The Exchange makes the contract adjustment so that the same level of investment is maintained before and after the ex-date. In other words, if you multiply the number of contracts by the adjusted contract size as well as by the adjusted exercise price, the total value should be the same as it was before the adjustment.

3. The expiry date is the specified time over which the option exists

Every option expires on the Thursday preceding the last Friday of the month, as long as both the Thursday and Friday are business days. If there is a public holiday on the last Friday of the month, you might find your option expiring on the Wednesday instead of the Thursday before.

Not every option trades in every calendar month. Each underlying share has what's called an expiry cycle. This shows you the range of months available for trading your particular shares via options, and also shows how far out in the future you can trade. Generally, option stocks follow one of three cycles:

1. January/April/July/October
2. February/May/August/November
3. March/June/September/December.

So, for example, ANZ follows the January/April/July/October expiry cycle. This means that if it were February, you would be able to choose from April, July, and October ANZ options.

In addition, some shares have what's called a spot month for trading. This means they trade in the current month, even if it's not part of their cycle. Taking the quarterly expiry cycle as an example, if it were April, there would be an April/June/September/December option available. As it gets closer to the April expiry a May option would be listed, giving you a selection of May/June/September/December. Once May expires, there would be June/September/December only.

As a rule of thumb, most options can be traded up to nine months in advance, but be aware that in practice you'll find that most of the liquidity (that is, activity) is in the three-month timeframe, with little liquidity in the six- or nine-month periods.

The Exchange publishes a calendar to show expiries for the year and it's a good idea to get one. It will show you at a glance the trading cycle and expiry date for your particular option.

So by standardising the three major components of an option, the Exchange has created a market in which you can freely trade, knowing exactly what you're getting. Every ANZ JAN 1000 call option is the same as every other ANZ JAN 1000 call option. You may recall, however, that there is a fourth component to an option—the premium.

The Premium

 The premium is not set by the Exchange. By definition, it is agreed on by the buyer and seller of the option.

The premium is quoted on a cents per share basis, so to convert it to a dollar value payment all you have to do is multiply the premium by 1,000 (the number of underlying shares). So, if you are buying a call option with a premium quoted at 25¢ per share, the total premium value is $250.00 ($0.25 × 1,000).

The premium will fluctuate during the life of the option according to market forces. In order to understand these market forces and how they will affect your option, however, you first need to understand a little more about the two sides of the equity call option.

3 THE EQUITY CALL OPTION DEFINED

Chapter objectives:

- Define an equity call option
- Define the two components of a call premium
- Describe the effect of different pricing factors on the time premium
- Provide practical ways of applying pricing theory
- Discuss the use of pricing models.

Earlier, you read a generic definition of an option. Now it's time to look specifically at equity call options.

Defining the Equity Call

A call option gives the taker the right, but not the obligation, to buy a standard quantity of shares at the exercise price, on or before the expiry date.

If the taker exercises his or her right to buy, the writer is required to sell a standard quantity of shares at the exercise price.

Take, for example, a BHP JAN 900 call. This tells you that:

- the taker has the right to buy 1,000 BHP shares at the exercise price of $9.00 on any day, up until the expiry date in January; and

- the writer has an obligation to sell 1,000 BHP shares at $9.00 if the taker exercises his/her right.

Now, what if BHP were trading at $11.00—wouldn't you like to have a few of these taken call options in your portfolio? It would be great to be able to buy BHP for $2.00 less than everybody else in the market.

The only component missing from our example is the premium, and you know that the premium is agreed to between the taker and writer. So, if you decided you wanted to buy one of these options, how much would you be willing to pay for it? Or alternatively, if you wanted to write one of these options, how much premium would you need to receive for incurring the obligation to sell BHP at $2.00 less than the current market price?

The Advantage of Buying Shares at a Lower Price than the Rest of the Market—Intrinsic Value

Before you answer these questions, let's take a step back from our BHP example. Let's say that you've been watching BHP for some time now, and feel that you would like to buy 1,000 shares. Unfortunately, your money is tied up in fixed interest for the next three months and you cannot withdraw it. Your concern is that by the time your money is free, BHP will have risen substantially and it will cost you more to enter the market. What you'd like to do is lock in a price for your BHP shares today. What do you do?

With BHP at $11.00, you decide to buy three different call options: a 1050, an 1100 and an 1150, giving you the right but no obligation to buy 1,000 BHP shares for $10.50, $11.00, or $11.50 each through exercise. Your three call options might look something like Figure 3.1, below.

Figure 3.1
BHP Call Option

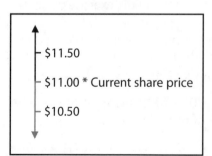

$11.50

$11.00 * Current share price

$10.50

Now, everyone else in the market must pay $11.00 for their shares, but since you bought options, you have a choice. You can decide to pay $10.50, $11.00 or $11.50 for your shares through exercising an option. Knowing that the first rule of successful trading in the sharemarket is 'buy low and sell high', which one would you exercise? The 1050 call, because by exercising your right to buy BHP for $10.50, you have paid 50¢ less than the rest of the market. In other words, you have a 50¢ advantage over everyone else, and this 50¢ is what is called **intrinsic value**.

> Intrinsic value is the option's real value. It is the advantage you would obtain through exercise, the profit through exercise of the option (excluding the premium paid) if you immediately sold your shares at the current share price. When you can pay less for your shares than the current market price through exercising your call, you have intrinsic value.

Is there any intrinsic value in the BHP 1100 call, or the 1150 call? The answer is no. The 1050 call is the only one with real value or profit through exercise, because it is the only option that allows you to 'buy low', i.e. lower than the current market price. In other words, a call option only has intrinsic value when its exercise price is lower than the current share price.

As the share price moves higher and higher past the exercise price, the option's intrinsic value increases with it. This is one reason why as the share price rises, call option premiums rise with it (all things being equal).

In-, At- and Out-of-the-Money

Okay, time for some more jargon:

- A call option that has an exercise price below the current share price has intrinsic value and is referred to as being **in-the-money**. You've probably heard the jingle, "I'm in the money"—well, that's what it means when your option has intrinsic value.
- A call option that is at the current share price is referred to as being **at-the-money**.
- A call option that has an exercise price above the current share price, and therefore no advantage through exercise, is referred to as being **out-of-the-money**. (See Figure 3.2, right.)

These terms are extremely important, because the first question your broker is going to

Figure 3.2
Call Option Exercise Prices

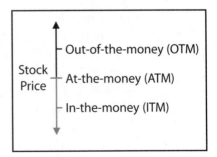

ask you when you say you want to buy a call option is, do you want to be in-, at- or out-of-the-money? These terms describe how close your particular option is to the current share price, and therefore how close it is to having any real value through exercise. Naturally, this relationship will change throughout the life of the option as the share price moves up and down.

You may hear brokers referring to an option as 'deep in-the-money'. This simply tells you that there is a lot of intrinsic value in the option. You may also hear an option being described as being 'close-to-the-money', 'around-the-money', or 'near-the-money'. This is because it is rare for an option to be exactly at-the-money—these terms let you know that the option is almost at-the-money. And if an option is deep out-of-the-money, it means it is extremely far away from the current share price and the chance of having intrinsic value.

Intrinsic Value + Time Value = the Premium

So you know that in-the-money calls have intrinsic, or real, value, while at-the-money and out-of-the-money calls do not. The question then becomes, what are you paying for when you buy an at- or out-of-the-money call option?

Going back to our BHP example where you were buying three different calls, let's say BHP is trading at $11.00 and the premiums are the following:

BHP JUL 1150	@	16¢
BHP JUL 1100	@	38¢
BHP JUL 1050	@	72¢

You can see immediately that the 1050 call has 50¢ intrinsic value. So what is the other 22¢ that you are paying? The answer is time value.

 You are paying for time. Remember, by definition a call option gives you the right to buy shares for a specified period of time. The longer that time is, the more time value there is in an option, and therefore the more you will pay for your option.

Since at-the-money and out-of-the-money options do not contain intrinsic value, all you are paying for is time. For the moment, you can think of time value very loosely as potential for profit in the future. In other words, these two options have no real value, so all you are paying for is the potential that they will have real value at some point in their life.

The Spread of Time

Looking at the intrinsic and time value of the three BHP calls, you can see the following:

Stock	Expiry	Exercise Price	Premium	Intrinsic Value	Time Value
BHP	JUL	1150 (OTM)	16¢	Nil	6¢
BHP	JUL	1100 (ATM)	38¢	Nil	38¢
BHP	JUL	1050 (ITM)	72¢	50¢	22¢

Look at the time value column. What do you notice? The at-the-money calls have the highest time value of all three series. This is true for all options. So, if time value is loosely 'potential for profit in the future', the market is telling you that the best potential is in the at-the-money option. Why isn't it in the in-the-money option? Because the return on the in-the-money option is less than the return on the at-the-money. You'll learn more about this later on, but for the moment, you're going to have to trust me on it.

As Time Goes By

As Dooley Wilson sang in Casablanca, "A kiss is still a kiss… as time goes by", but unfortunately an option is not still an option as time goes by—after all, it won't exist after expiry. So what happens to it?

You know so far that:

Option premium = Intrinsic value + Time value

You also know that if there is no intrinsic value in an option, there is only time value. The more time there is until expiry, the more time value there is. So, it follows that the less time there is until expiry, the less time value there is in the option. In other words, if you buy a nine-month option today, after one month has passed, eight months of time value is left. How much time value is in an option at expiry? Zero. So something happens to that option's time value between day one when there is nine months of time, and expiry day when there is no time value left. That something is what is referred to as **time decay**.

 Options are wasting assets. Through nothing but the passage of time, options will lose value. Since there is no time value at expiry, an option is only worth its intrinsic value. If there is no intrinsic value in the option at expiry, the option expires worthless.

This means you cannot afford to pop options in the bottom drawer with your shares and forget about them. You must monitor your calls daily to see the effect on your premiums.

Time decay can be particularly vicious in quiet markets. Not only is it vicious, it is also quite cunning, because it does not decay at a constant rate. As a rule of thumb, you will lose approximately one-third of your time value in the first half of the option's life, and two-thirds in the second half. This means that time decay accelerates as it gets closer and closer to expiry. In real terms, in the last four to six weeks of the option's life there is usually little if any time value left, unless the market price is rising strongly (see Figure 3.3, below).

Figure 3.3
Call Option Time Decay

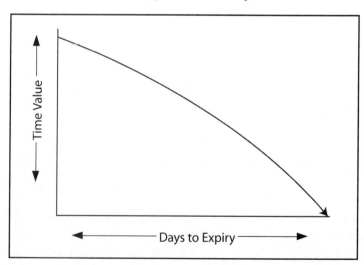

Time value reflects what the market is willing to pay for the right to buy shares by a set date in the future. The more time left on an option, the greater the probability that the share price will move favourably and the option will have intrinsic value. As it gets closer to expiry that probability becomes increasingly less likely; hence the rapid decay of the time premium.

The Third Dimension of Options Trading—Volatility

So far you can see the impact of the share price and time on your option premiums. But options trade in three main dimensions: price, time and **volatility**. So how does volatility affect your call option premiums?

Firstly, let's define volatility.

Volatility refers to the size and frequency of the underlying share price movements. It is a measure of how far a share price is likely to move (that is, up or down) around an average price over a specified period of time.

If a share price is moving up and down in large, rapid movements over a period of time, it is described as being volatile, or having high volatility. It is important to understand that volatility is non-directional. In other words, a stock can be described as being volatile when there is no clear trend up or down over a period of time. Most people think of News Corp as an example of a volatile stock.

Volatility is expressed as a percentage. The higher the percentage, the higher the volatility is in the underlying shares, and therefore the greater the movements are likely to be in that stock.

Let's look at an example. Let's say XYZ stock shows a volatility of 10 per cent over the last 12 months. Its average price over this time is $4.00. This means that on average, XYZ has moved between a range of $3.60 (40¢ down from its average price) and $4.40 (40¢ up from its average price). You can see from this example that volatility gives an indication of the price range a share is likely to trade within. Two words are stressed here: 'indication' and 'likely'. It doesn't mean it *cannot* trade outside this range, but it does give you a good indication that it probably won't. This is important when you are deciding to buy an in-, at-, or out-of-the-money call option, because it gives you a clue as to how far the share price can move within a certain space of time. (More about this later.)

So how does volatility affect your call premiums? As a buyer of a call option, you love volatility. Why? Because if the share price is moving up and down in large, quick movements, there's a good chance the share price will go up and up and up and you'll make a profit from your option. It's no good to you if the share price stays flat, because what happens to your option in a flat market? Time decay. When you buy a call you need the market to rise strongly to counteract the effect of time decay on your premium.

As volatility in the underlying share price increases, more buyers come into the market, thereby driving call premiums up with the demand. So, as a buyer of a call option, you look for low volatility to buy your option (that is, buy when the premium will be cheaper), and your expectation is for volatility to increase or at least stay the same over the life of your option. If volatility decreases, your option will lose premium value.

Price, time and volatility have the greatest impact on call option premiums. However, there are two other factors you need to take into account when pricing the premium on your option—dividends and interest rates.

The Impact of Dividends on Call Premiums

As a share trader you no doubt know that when a share goes ex-dividend, the share price falls. Since there is a direct relationship between the movement of the share price and the movement of the corresponding call, if the stock falls in price the call premium falls with it (all things being equal). This means that if there is a dividend due on the shares underlying your particular call, the price of the call will be lower than if there were no dividend due.

Be aware that the expectation of the dividend is factored into the price of the call from day one of its trading, so you will not see a fall in the call premium the day after the shares go ex-dividend—well, not due to the shares going ex-dividend, anyway. If this weren't the case, knowing that the share price (and therefore call price) would fall as the shares went ex-dividend, no-one would buy a call before a dividend was due.

Also bear in mind that if you wish to exercise your call to receive the dividend due on the shares, you must exercise while the shares are listed cum-dividend—that is, with the dividend attached.

Interest Rates and Call Premiums

To understand the effect interest rates have on call premiums, you need to have an understanding of how your choice of entering the sharemarket impacts on the cost-effectiveness of your trading.

For example, let's say you want to buy 1,000 BHP shares today because you believe today's price of $11.00 is low. What can you do? Clearly, you can buy the 1,000 shares at $11.00 today, thereby choosing to take $11,000 from your bank account and buying the shares (disregarding commissions and other costs of trading). Alternatively, you can take a much smaller amount from your bank account, let's say $1,000, to buy a BHP 1100 call option, giving you the right to buy your 1,000 BHP shares for $11.00 each but not having to pay for them until you exercise in the future. Think of all that interest you're saving by leaving most of your money in the bank and buying the call option!

For this reason it is said that the call buyer has an interest rate saving or advantage through buying the call instead of the stock. But guess what? There's no such thing as a free lunch! If you have an advantage, it means that someone else has the disadvantage, and they're not going to be happy about that. Since the writer of the call misses out on putting the $11,000 into the bank and earning the interest until you decide to exercise and pay for the shares, he or she is going to demand you pay a higher premium for your call as interest rates rise.

Interest rates can have a small or large impact on call premiums, depending on the interest rate climate at the time. For example, if interest rates were around 3 or 4 per cent, the impact would be small. Alternatively, if interest rates were to climb up to 18 per cent, the impact would be much greater. Generally, interest rates are relatively slow to change over a period of time. However, the rule of thumb is the higher the interest rate, the higher call premiums will be for that option.

The Impact of Price Factors—Using Pricing Models

You've read how each price factor individually impacts on your call option (summarised in Table 3.1, overleaf), however, bear in mind that at any point in time any or all of these factors may be changing. So if the share price rises you might think that your call option will automatically rise with it, since that's the theory. In reality, you might find your call falls in value due to time decay or falling volatility, or simply declining demand.

Clearly, you don't have any control over what happens once you are in the market, but what you do have control over is the price you pay before you get into it. It's stating the obvious, but the rule here is don't pay too much for your option. So how can you tell what an option is worth? Knowing all the factors that impact on option prices, how do you use this information to tell if the market price is fair and that the option is not over-priced?

Table 3.1
Impact of Pricing Factors

Increase In	Movement in Call Premium
Stock Price	Increase
Exercise Price	Decrease
Time to Expiry	Increase
Volatility	Increase
Dividends	Decrease
Interest Rates	Increase

Pricing models are one solution used by traders. Some of the best-known are the Black-Scholes, Binomial, and Cox Ross Rubenstein Trinomial models.

Basically, a pricing model is an economic formula that enables you to input the various pricing factors (share price, exercise price, time to expiry, volatility, etc.) and calculate the fair value, or theoretical real value, for the option. You can then see if the option is trading at its fair value in the market, or whether it is over- or under-priced.

The basic rule is, you buy the under-priced option and sell the over-priced option. Alternatively, if you're not happy about writing options, you at least would not buy the over-priced option. So the pricing model is an early warning of paying too much for your option.

A word of warning is needed here. Before you stop reading and rush out to buy a pricing model, thinking they are one of the Holy Grails of trading, you need to be aware that it's not that easy. For a start, while certain pricing factors do not change over the life of the option (for example, the exercise price and dividends), others, like volatility and interest rates, may change. What this means is if you are buying a three-month call option today and using a pricing model to price it, you have to decide what the level of volatility and so on is expected to be for the next three months. That's easy, you say, because you can look up volatility for the last three months and plug that into the model. But what if the rest of the market believes volatility will be higher than that, and is therefore pricing the options higher in the market than you are?

 Pricing models can only give you a guide to the fair value of the option, since some of the inputs are subjective. It doesn't necessarily mean you shouldn't use them. Use them if they work for you, don't use them if they don't work for you.

Note that if you do decide to use a pricing model, you don't have to buy one, since you can find them readily on industry websites. Different pricing models will give slightly different fair value calculations, so be careful if you are comparing your calculation with that of someone else. You must know the pricing model they have used to effectively compare the results. In addition, the level of volatility used in the calculation can greatly affect the outcome—because the option premium increases with volatility, if others use a higher volatility measure in their calculations they will automatically get a higher fair value for the same option. You must find out what level of volatility was used to calculate the fair value.

Okay, you know that different people will have differing views about the level of volatility in the same underlying stock over the same period of time. This is why markets exist, because we all have different opinions. So, if you are going to compare your fair value calculation, you are going to need to know the value everyone else is placing on volatility. But with thousands of people trading in the same stock every day, you cannot possibly ask each one of them what they think volatility will be for that stock over the next, say, three months. How can you tell the value the market is placing on volatility? The answer is to work backwards to calculate the **implied volatility**.

 Implied volatility is a measure of how volatile the whole market believes that particular stock will be for the remaining life of the option.

In other words, looking at the pricing model, if you know what the fair value is, you can work out the level of volatility needed to make that fair value. So, using the market price as the fair value, you can calculate the level of implied volatility in the market.

This is where pricing models can be really useful. Bear in mind though, that while this is a helpful way of using pricing models, you can also find implied volatility measures in the financial press. (See Chapter 13, 'Using Financial Information to Optimise Trading', for some tips on how to interpret and use implied volatility measures.)

If pricing models are only a guide anyway, how do you know how much a call option is *really* worth? Let's face it, you don't. If you want to know how much your house is worth, a real estate agent can give you an estimate and you can see what other houses in the area are selling for, but you can't really tell what it's worth until you go to auction it in the market. In the same way with your option, you can't really find out what it's worth until you go to the market— that is, you look at a price screen or ask your broker. Ultimately, an option is worth whatever the market is willing to pay for it.

Still worried you might pay too much? Okay, then you need to understand more about the way the market works and how the professional market prices options. You might want to read Chapter 11, 'Making Markets', next. It contains a few tips on how to evaluate whether your option is too expensive and on how to avoid paying too much. Otherwise, stay with me, and we'll look next at the most commonly used strategy in the world of options— the bought call option.

4 THE BOUGHT CALL

BUYING EXPOSURE TO SHARES FOR A FRACTION OF THE PRICE

Chapter objectives:

- Discuss the three ways of exiting a trade
- Summarise three reasons why you would buy a call
- Introduce the concept of delta as a measure of risk/return
- Provide a method of calculating return on investment
- Differentiate the two elements of risk
- Discuss option selection based on price and time
- Construct the bought call payoff diagram
- Provide practical ways of interpreting and applying the payoff diagram
- Discuss basic entry and exit rules.

So far you know:

- The call taker, or buyer, has the right to buy 1,000 shares for a set price over a set period of time.
- Calls increase in value as the underlying share price increases (all things being equal).
- Calls decrease in value as the option gets closer to expiry (all things being equal).
- Calls increase in value as volatility increases (all things being equal).
- At expiry, a call is only worth its intrinsic value.

Clearly, you buy a call when you think the share price is going to rise. In other words, you are bullish on the underlying share price, and because of the effect of time decay, probably 'aggressively' bullish.

Obviously, if you get it wrong and the share price falls, your call is going to fall in premium value. And you know that by expiry, the call will be worthless if there is no intrinsic value. So how do you make a profit or loss once you have bought your call?

Two Ways to Exit and Make a Profit

When you buy a call option, you can make a profit either through exercise or through selling the call back onto the market for a higher premium.

1. Exercising to buy the underlying shares

If you want to own the underlying shares, you can exercise the call on any day up to and including the expiry day. Clearly, exercise will only be to your advantage if the share price has risen over your exercise price—that is, you have intrinsic value in your call. There's nothing stopping you from exercising an out-of-the-money call option, but it's a fairly silly thing to do, since you could buy the shares for a lower price in the market.

2. Selling the call back onto the market

If the share price is rising and your call premium is worth more than when you bought it, you can sell the call back onto the market. Your profit will be the difference between the buying price and the selling price of the call (less any cost of trading).

> When you place the order to sell with your broker, it is important to tell him or her that it is an order to close out, or liquidate, your bought position. In this way, you ensure that the two orders cancel each other out, and you won't end up holding 'back to back' contracts (that is, one bought and one sold call option) in your portfolio.

Obviously if your call has fallen in value, you can still sell the option, but it will be at a loss. This might be appropriate to limit losses in your trading. (More about this later.) So which do you do? Exercise or sell the option? The rule of thumb here is, you only exercise if you want to own the underlying shares.

> If you only want to make a profit out of the premium movement and have no intention of owning the shares, you are always better off selling the call. The reason is, when you exercise your call you lose any time value left on the option and you only recoup the intrinsic value. Remember, by definition, intrinsic value is the profit through exercise—and that's all you get.

An example will demonstrate this. Let's say you buy a BHP JAN 1100 at 38¢. The share price rises strongly over the next month, BHP is now trading at $11.50 and the call premium is now trading at 62¢. This premium represents 50¢ of intrinsic value and 12¢ of time.

You decide to exercise your right to buy BHP for $11.00 while it is at $11.50. If you exercise and immediately sell the shares, you would make 50¢ per share; that is, the intrinsic value less the initial cost of 38¢—your profit would be 12¢. Alternatively, if you simply sold the call back into the market, you would make 62¢ less the original cost of 38¢, or a profit of 24¢. The extra 12¢ represents the time value left on the call. Not only do you make the extra profit in time value, your transaction costs will be much lower than they would be if you simply bought the shares.

The majority of call buyers in the market exit by closing out the position, rather than by exercising to buy shares. Most Exchanges quote that somewhere between 4 per cent and 15 per cent of options are exercised.

The Third Way to Exit

So, you can exercise your call or you can sell it back onto the market. There is also a third thing you can do—you can allow your option to expire.

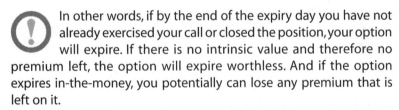 In other words, if by the end of the expiry day you have not already exercised your call or closed the position, your option will expire. If there is no intrinsic value and therefore no premium left, the option will expire worthless. And if the option expires in-the-money, you potentially can lose any premium that is left on it.

Even if the option is only worth a few cents prior to expiry, it is almost always better to close your position with some premium left than to allow it to expire worthless. Only 'almost always', I hear you say? Yes, because if there is only 2¢ of premium left on your option and the cost of closing it (commission, etc.) is more than 2¢, you would be better to let it expire. Otherwise, close it out and take whatever's left of the premium.

Be aware that the Exchange offers an automatic exercise facility to brokers. This means that if an option is a particular amount in-the-money at expiry, and has not yet been closed, the option will be automatically exercised. The parameters for automatic exercise change regularly, so it is important to either visit the Exchange website to see what the parameters are, or alternatively, ask your broker. In addition, not all brokers offer the facility, so you also need to ask this before opening an account with a particular broker.

Three Reasons for Buying a Call Option

There are three main reasons you might decide to buy a call option:

1. You want to lock in a price to buy shares at a future date

As previously discussed, there may be times when you want to add certain shares to your portfolio but don't have the money to pay for them today. You can buy the call option at the exercise price you're happy with, and have the time to decide if you want to buy the shares. Remember, you've paid the premium upfront, so this cost must be added onto your final purchase price.

If you want to purchase the shares, you must exercise your option by the expiry date. Clearly, the only advantage to you through exercise is if the share price has risen above your exercise price.

2. You want to speculate on an expected price movement in the underlying shares

You may not want to have ownership of the underlying shares, you might just want to make a profit out of an expected share price rise. By buying a call and selling it for a higher premium, you are able to take advantage of your market view without actually entering the sharemarket.

3. You want to gain short-term leveraged exposure to the underlying shares

Similar to point two above, by buying a call option without the view to exercise, you gain exposure to share price movements over the life of the option. In this way, you can effectively switch exposure to a stock you feel will perform better over a short period of time, without the high cost (share cost, commission, etc.) of trading in the actual sharemarket. This is a popular strategy with fund managers, who can find the cost of switching from one underperforming share to another better-performing share excessive. In other words, if they can get similar exposure to a share for a cheaper outlay, it improves their returns.

Right, now you know:

- why you want to buy the call—that is, you're bullish on the underlying stock

- your reason for buying it—that is, you want ownership of the shares or you just want exposure to the share price movements
- whether you will exercise it or sell it back onto the market.

What you don't know is which option you're going to buy. Will you buy in-, at- or out-of-the-money? Will you buy a short-dated or longer-dated call? To answer that, you need to know one more thing about the way call option premiums change over the life of the option.

A Measure of Risk/Reward—Delta

Let's say you are looking at XYZ stock at $4.00 and considering the following calls:

ITM 350	@	72¢
ATM 400	@	38¢
OTM 450	@	16¢

You know that each of these calls will give you exposure to 1,000 XYZ shares, and each will rise when the share price rises (all things being equal). So which would you buy? Would you rather pay 16¢, 38¢ or 72¢ to get your exposure to 1,000 XYZ shares? You might be tempted to say 16¢, since this gives you the same exposure to the 1,000 shares as the more expensive options. But does it? Would you expect each option to rise by the same amount when the share price rises, let's say, by $1.00? To answer that, you need to understand the concept of an option's delta.

 Delta is a measure of how much the premium will move when the share price moves. It tells you how sensitive your particular option will be to price movements in the underlying share.

The calculation for delta is simply:

$$\frac{\text{Change in call premium}}{\text{Change in share price}}$$

Delta for calls is therefore expressed on a scale between 0 and 1. A delta of 1 means your option will move one-for-one with the share, or will move 100 per cent in line with the share price movement. So, if the share price moves up $1.00, you would expect your call premium to rise by $1.00. A delta of 0 means your option will have no movement when the share price moves.

> As a rough guide, an out-of-the-money call has a delta somewhere around 0.1 or 0.2 (depending on how deep out-of-the-money it is), and will change by approximately 10 per cent to 20 per cent of the share price change. An at-the-money call has a delta around 0.5, and will change by approximately 50 per cent of the share price change. An in-the-money call has a delta around 0.7 or 0.8 (depending on how deep in-the-money it is), and will change by somewhere around 70 per cent to 80 per cent of the share price change. Figure 4.1, below, shows this visually.

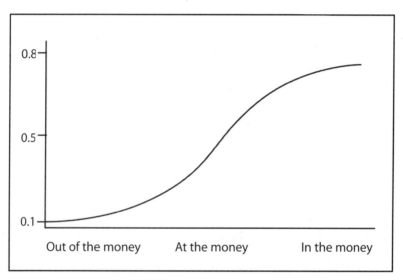

Figure 4.1
Call Options Delta

As a call gets deeper into the money, its delta approaches 1. In other words, it mirrors the price movements of the underlying share. At this point the option will generally lose any remaining time value and will be valued by its intrinsic value alone. If this were not the case, the option would have more value to it than the underlying share!

Does knowing an option's delta change your answer to the question of which option you would buy? Your first thought might have been to buy the cheap out-of-the-money, but knowing that its delta is small, and therefore you can expect a small change in the premium as the share price rises, would you still choose this option?

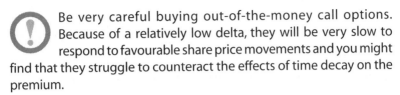Be very careful buying out-of-the-money call options. Because of a relatively low delta, they will be very slow to respond to favourable share price movements and you might find that they struggle to counteract the effects of time decay on the premium.

Now that I've told you to be careful buying out-of-the-money calls, I'm going to show you that out of all the option series, out-of-the-money calls will give you the highest return of the lot.

Which Option to Buy? The Return on Your Investment

Okay, so making profits is great, but the reason you are trading options is to increase your returns. How do you make sure you are optimising your share trading, and getting the best return?

Return on investment is calculated by using the following formula:

$$\frac{\text{Profit on trade}}{\text{Initial premium}} \times 100 \times \frac{365 \text{ (days in the year)}}{\text{Trading days}}$$

This calculation annualises the return, and this means you can use it to compare with other potential returns (for example, bank returns) to see exactly what you could be achieving for the year. For example, let's say that you buy an XYZ 1000 call option for 50¢, and after 87 trading days, your option is closed out for 62¢. Your return on investment would be:

$$\frac{0.12}{0.50} \times 100 \times \frac{365}{87} = 100.7\%$$

So what is a good return? And how do you 'optimise' returns? Only you can answer that, bearing in mind that the higher the return you want, the higher the risk you will probably have to assume. One way to gauge a good return is to check and see what the fund managers are currently returning. Is anyone returning 120 per cent on his or her share portfolio? Or 50 per cent? If you see the funds managers returning 10 or 12 per cent, more than likely you won't be able to do better than that in the climate at the time. If you can, it may be because you are assuming a lot more risk in the market.

Let's get back to your dilemma of buying your call option. Using the above three calls, we're going to assume the following:

- XYZ shares are trading at $4.00 when you buy the three calls.
- You buy a 350, 400 and 450 call.
- At the expiry, XYZ shares are trading at $5.00.
- You are right about XYZ going up in price, and all three options expire in-the-money, or with intrinsic value.

By showing all three options with a profit, you can compare the returns you get, and therefore get a feel for how trading can be optimised:

	350 CALL	400 CALL	450 CALL
Premium	$0.72	$0.38	$0.16
Intrinsic	$1.50	$1.00	$0.50
Profit	$0.78	$0.62	$0.34
Return (not annualised)	108%	163%	212.5%

The first thing you see is that the greatest profit is made with the in-the-money option. This will always be the case since it has the biggest delta, and therefore will move more closely with the underlying share price movement. But it's not hip-dollar profit that necessarily gives us the best return. In other words, because of the high cost of the in-the-money premium (due to the fact that you're paying a high cost for existing intrinsic value), your return is actually the lowest of all the series. Looking along the column, you see that the return increases as the exercise price goes further out-of-the-money. In fact, the out-of-the-money option has the greatest return of all the option series. And I've just told you to be careful trading them!

Before you race out to start trading out-of-the-money calls, let's take a step back and look at why they have the greatest return. Out-of-the-money calls have the greatest return because the initial premium is so small. However, you only achieve the return if you get it right and the share price rises well above your exercise price by expiry. In other words, what would the return be if the share price were at $4.50 at option expiry? The out-of-the-money call would have no intrinsic value, no time value, and would expire worthless, giving you a negative return. Even though you were right and the share price went up, it didn't go up enough for your option to return a profit. This example shows you the two risks of trading options. One is the hip-pocket amount you can lose—that is, the premium. The other is the probability of losing it. It is vital that you factor in both when considering the total risk of trading.

This second risk is the one most traders ignore. I remember once hearing a broker tell his client that instead of buying the one at-the-money call for 38¢, they could instead buy two out-of-the-money calls for a total of 32¢. This broker went on to say that doing this would increase the return to a whopping 425 per cent and reduce their risk to only 32¢. However, it is not possible to increase your return without increasing your risk. What the broker had not factored in was the probability of his client losing the total premium. Obviously this part of risk is much higher in the out-of-the-moneys than the at-the-moneys.

> The at-the-money call has the highest return coupled with the best chance to get that return. This is what time value really represents. The market is telling you that it is pricing at-the-money calls with more time value than in- or out-of-the-money because they are worth more. Listen to the market.

This doesn't mean you should never trade out-of-the-money calls. Just be aware of the risks. They aren't a 'bargain', since there's no such thing in the market. You're paying less for them because they have less chance of making a profit—that's what the smaller premium represents. You need to be really bullish about a stock to consider out-of-the-moneys. I have seen clients buy them just because they couldn't afford to buy the at-the-money, and this is the wrong reason.

In real terms, you will find that most of the trading takes place in the at-the-money series of any stock. This gives you the added benefit of liquidity, providing a more efficient market and therefore more efficient pricing of the options. It also gives you an easier entry and exit, since it means more people will be interested in trading them.

Which Expiry to Buy? The Perils of Time

Okay, so you've decided to buy the at-the-money call. Great. But when you look at a price screen or pricing information in the newspaper you see several different expiry months listed. Which one should you trade?

Which expiry month you select will depend on:

- your view of the market. That is, when do you expect the share price move to happen—in the next few days, the next three months, the next six?
- how much time you can afford to buy
- how liquid the different expiry months are.

Generally, the most liquid expiry months are the spot month options and the three-month options. As you go further out to, say, nine months, you will probably find that there is little liquidity. This doesn't mean you shouldn't trade them, it just means the pricing won't be as efficient—you'll pay more to get in and will receive less to get out.

Three months may not sound like a long time, especially to someone who is used to long-term shareholding, however a lot can happen to an option premium in a short space of time.

Options should be used to give you short-term exposure to the underlying share price, not as a complete replacement to share buying. Be careful buying too much time. If you have a view that the share price will move but not for six months, you might be better off waiting three or four months before buying an option, or alternatively buying the shares outright. If nothing's going to happen to the share price during that time, something will happen to your option premium if you buy too early—and that something is time decay. Options should be used when your expectation is for a movement in the share price in the near future.

In addition, be careful of not buying enough time. Remember, time decay rapidly accelerates in the last four to six weeks of an option's life. It doesn't mean you shouldn't trade during this time, in fact, if you do you'll be buying calls which are quite cheap. But remember the two sides of risk. The risk in the last few weeks of an option's life is that if you get it wrong, the call will be really quick to lose value through time decay. You may not have time to take any defensive action to protect your premium.

So you've now chosen the exercise price and expiry of the call you want to buy. Before you buy it, you also want to know whether this represents a good choice in terms of risk/reward. How can you tell? One way is to have a look at its profit and loss profile.

The Option Payoff—Profit and Loss Profile for the Bought Call

A profit and loss profile, also called a payoff diagram or expiry diagram, is a snapshot at expiry of your particular option. It shows whether you will make a profit or loss on the trade (not including commissions and other costs of trading) according to where the share price is at expiry, and in relation to the exercise price and premium paid for your specific option. In other words, it looks purely at the intrinsic value of the option, since there is no time value left at that time.

Basically, the profile is drawn with the share price along the horizontal axis, potential profit above the zero on the vertical axis, and potential loss below the zero on the vertical axis (see Figure 4.2, overleaf). If you want to draw your option profile, you simply choose a share price, calculate whether your option has any intrinsic value at that price, and then subtract the premium paid. The resulting profit or loss is then plotted on the graph. After several points are plotted, you can then join the points to reveal the profile.

For example, let's say you buy one ABC MAR 400 call for 50¢. You do the following calculations:

Share Price at Expiry	Intrinsic Value	Premium	Profit/Loss
$3.00	Nil	$0.50	$0.50 loss
$3.50	Nil	$0.50	$0.50 loss
$4.00	Nil	$0.50	$0.50 loss
$4.50	$0.50	$0.50	Nil
$5.00	$1.00	$0.50	$0.50 profit
$6.00	$2.00	$0.50	$1.50 profit

Plotting the various profits and losses, and then joining the dots would result in the profile shown in Figure 4.2.

The profile for the bought call shows three really important things:

1. As the buyer of a call option, you can never lose more than the premium you pay

You can see from the above profile that no matter how far the share price falls, your loss is capped at 50¢. The share price could fall all the way to zero, and you would still only lose your initial premium of 50¢. This is one of the call option's biggest advantages over buying shares—the bought call has limited risk, limited to the amount of premium paid for it.

Figure 4.2
The Bought Call—ABC MAR 400 Call Bought for 50¢

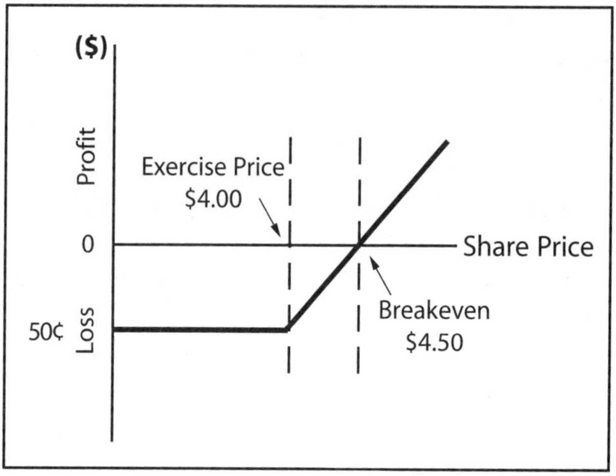

2. The breakeven on the trade is at the exercise price plus the premium paid

In other words, as the share price rises above the exercise price you start to have intrinsic value on your call. However, you must recoup the premium you've paid before you can make a profit.

3. As the share price rises, you have the ability to make unlimited profit

You can see from the above example that once the share price rises above the breakeven point, you make a larger and larger profit as the share price continues to rise. If, for example, the share price is at $1,000 at expiry, you would make a profit of $995.50.

> Just a word of warning. The profit and loss diagram does not include time value, or show profit and loss during the life of the option. It doesn't mean that you should hold an option until expiry—quite the opposite. Remember that time decay rapidly increases during the last four to six weeks. The only reason option profiles are shown at expiry is because the value of the option can be easily calculated without the use of a pricing model. Usually the worst thing you can do is hold an option until expiry. (More about this later.)

The profit and loss diagram is a good way of seeing at a glance the potential profit and loss for your particular option. More importantly, it gives you a clear picture of the second aspect of risk: the probability of making that profit or loss. Let's see how.

The Myth of Unlimited Reward

You can see from Figure 4.2 that a bought call option shows a risk/reward of limited risk/unlimited reward. In other words, you're risking a very small premium for a potentially very large reward. This looks pretty much like a dream come true, doesn't it? Let's examine it for a moment. Limited risk and unlimited reward. What does 'unlimited reward' sound like to you? Does it sound like you could make a fortune from one trade?

 I'd like to pull you back from the idea that 'unlimited reward' means a fortune. The reality of buying call options is that somewhere around 80 per cent of option buyers will lose their money.

That's not my statistic, that's what the Exchange usually quotes. Anecdotal evidence from around the world indicates that this statistic is internationally accepted by most exchanges. However, my experience in broking is that it's more like 95 per cent—and that's not just my clients, that's talking to brokers over the last 15 years and hearing their experiences with their clients.

So why do so many option buyers lose their money? I believe one of the reasons is the myth of unlimited reward. If you tell a client that it is possible to make unlimited profit then he or she isn't going to be satisfied making a small profit. This means that most call buyers stay in the market too long, not taking what they consider to be too small a profit, and then generally losing everything when the market turns against them.

 The profit potential for a bought call is not unlimited. It is simply undefined at the start of the trade. In reality, the profit potential is definitely limited by two things: time and volatility. In other words, the amount the share price can rise is limited by the time remaining on the option, and by the amount it generally moves around.

For example, looking at a $4.00 stock, what is the probability that it will be at $1,000 within the next three months? Probably pretty close to zero. Or $50? Or $10? In order to answer that, you need to have a look at its volatility for the last three months. This will give you a good indication of how far that stock is likely to go over the next three months. Again, I stress two words: 'indication' and 'likely'.

It doesn't mean the price can't move outside this range, we are only looking at probabilities here. If the last three months' volatility is 10 per cent, you would expect your $4.00 stock could move up or down by 10 per cent, or 40¢. This means your $4.00 stock could go up to $4.40. Knowing this, would you still buy your 400 call for 50¢? Probably not. On the other hand, if the volatility was 50 per cent, it would mean the stock could go up to $6.00, and your 400 call could return a profit of $1.50. Your risk/reward would then be 50 ÷ $1.50, or 1/3. Quite acceptable, and a lot more realistic than the expectation of an unlimited reward.

So, looking at the second aspect of risk (that is, the probability of making a profit or loss), it is important for you to define that undefined profit potential at the start of the trade. This means you will have a more realistic risk/reward scenario, get an indication of whether your option will be profitable at all and be more prepared to take a profit based on this.

Potential Risk, the Breakeven and Volatility

The premium immediately tells you the loss potential on the option. In other words, the hip-pocket risk of trading is limited by the premium paid for the option. The breakeven point gives you an indication of how high the share price has to move before you make a profit. It also shows the total cost of buying shares through exercise of the option.

Reviewing volatility together with the premium risk and the breakeven point is a useful way of deciding which option series to buy—that is, whether you buy at- or out-of-the-money. Knowing that the breakeven for buying a call option is the exercise price plus the premium, you can calculate breakevens for several different exercise prices. Using historical volatility measures over the same period can tell you whether the share price is likely to rise above each breakeven, and therefore which exercise price is more likely to be profitable for you.

For example:

	Exercise Price	Premium	Breakeven
ABC MAR	400 Call	38¢	$4.38
ABC MAR	450 Call	16¢	$4.66

It might be tempting to buy the out-of-the-money call because your hip-pocket risk is less than for the at-the-money call. However, the breakeven for an out-of-the-money is much higher than for the at-the-money. This means that the probability of returning a profit is less, since the share price has to rise much higher before you start returning a profit. So, apart from delta, this is another reason why you have to be far more bullish if you're buying out-of-the-money calls.

Getting into the Successful 20 per cent

Hopefully you're still reading and haven't been put off by the statistics that around 80 per cent of option buyers lose their money. The point of reading this book is to help you get into the remaining 20 per cent who make highly leveraged returns. The way you do that is to understand what goes wrong and how you can prevent it.

Most investors start off their trading by buying call options. Generally, share investors are used to buying shares when they think the price will rise, and doing nothing if the market is flat or falling. So, the idea of buying something is highly ingrained. The bought call is also one of the easiest strategies to understand, and has the added benefit of a known and limited risk. You can sleep at night without the fear of unlimited risk.

Let's use our previous example of buying an at-the-money ABC MAR 400 call for 38¢. The first thing your broker will want to know is if you are happy about the risk. He/she will ask something like, are you happy to risk the premium and lose 38¢ on the trade? Firstly, your broker is trying to put your mind at ease by reminding you that you cannot lose more than the premium, and secondly, he/she is trying to make sure you understand your full risk. Now you know you should only trade with risk capital—that is, money you can afford to lose—so you answer, yes, I'm happy to lose 38¢. You pay the premium to your broker, and sit back to see what's going to happen to your call.

The first thing I would like to say to you is, do not tell your broker or yourself that you are happy to lose the premium. The brain is a funny thing, it processes information literally. If you tell yourself you are happy to lose the money, you are telling your brain that you don't mind losing it. And guess what? You probably will.

Please, do not be happy to lose your premium. Even though you have limited risk when you buy a call, you should limit this even further than the full premium amount. (More about this later.) Tell your brain that you want to protect your full premium and you will be more likely to take defensive action if the market moves against you. It is really important to remind yourself that the money is not gone yet. The pain of losing your money occurs at the point of transferring it to your broker—after that, you don't feel a thing. Yet it is, in fact, invested, and the most important thing for you to do is protect your investment.

So how do you limit losses and make sure you maximise profits?

Defining Exit Rules

As a share trader, you are probably used to carefully analysing your entry rules for buying shares. You might use fundamental indicators, possibly some technical indicators to finely tune your price range, and then you place your order to buy. What happens then? If you are a long-term holder, probably nothing. More than likely you sit on your shares and only sell them for cash flow or if you decide the long-term growth would be better in another share.

With options, it is really important to define your exit rules at the same time you define your entry rules. Sounds backwards, doesn't it? I mean, why would you decide when to get out before you get in? The answer is, in order to minimise your losses and maximise your profits. Let's face it, most investors spend all their time analysing entry points and very little time analysing exit points, and yet when you think about it, the exits are when you make the profit or loss on the trade.

Exit points are more important than your entries. If you spent no time on entry analysis, maybe flipped a coin to decide which stock you would buy, and then spent lots of time analysing your exit points, overall you would be more successful in your trading than doing it the other way around.

Remember that options give you exposure to the underlying shares for a period of time. During this time, the share price movement, volatility and time decay will have a huge impact on the value of your option.

Unlike shares, with options you do not have the luxury of months, weeks or even days to decide whether you want to exit your trade. I have seen out-of-the-money gold options turn into in-the-money

42

options 10 minutes before expiry. So it is vital that you are able to make quick decisions about exiting, and the best way to do this is to know when you are getting out before you get in. Then the decision is based on clear objectives that you have set for the trade, rather than a knee-jerk reaction to a share price movement. Over time, this means an average lower level of loss across your trading rather than large, erratic losses that quickly reduce your capital. (For more about this see Chapter 14, 'Managing Your Position and Your Money'.)

So how do you decide when to exit your option?

Loss Targets

Okay, so no-one wants to think about taking a loss on their option. We're all optimists, right? We buy a call option because we have a view on the market, an expectation about what's going to happen to the share price, and that expectation is that it will rise. Our ego wants to believe that we will be right.

One of the hardest things you'll ever do is realise a loss on your option. Since human nature is to avoid the hard things in life, you might find yourself in typical avoidance behaviour, doing anything to escape the fact that you are wrong and you have to take a loss. When an option expires worthless it's usually painless to your ego—you've already parted with the money, and you don't have to do anything like placing an order with your broker in order to make the loss concrete. It just 'disappears' out of your account as if it never existed.

I know this is the typical behaviour of call buyers from over four years spent in retail broking, and from the fact that at least 80 per cent of option buyers lose their money. What happens to them?

Let's say you've bought your first option, an at-the-money XYZ JUN 400 call for 38¢. You know you have limited risk and unlimited profit, and that your breakeven is at $4.38. You have three months to see what's going to happen to the underlying stock and to your option. Now what?

Let's say that the market stays flat for a while, nothing's really changed except your option has lost some value through time decay. It's now trading at 34¢. You know you have another two and a half months of time left, so you wait to see what's going to happen. Another two weeks go by, the share price falls slightly—nothing too dramatic—and your option is now worth 26¢. You've paid for three months of time and you want to get your money's worth, so you decide to wait to see what's going to happen. After all, not a lot has changed, you haven't been proven wrong yet, and the share price could move up substantially over the next two months. By the end of the next month, XYZ shares are trading at $3.20 and your option is worth 14¢.

Here's a dilemma. You can see that the share price hasn't really changed that much and that time decay is what has eaten into your premium. You still believe that XYZ shares are going to rise over the next month, and you're afraid that as soon as you exit your trade the share price will rocket up. You decide to wait. The next day, XYZ shares go up to $4.00. You were right! You're so glad you kept your position. You check with your broker to find out what it's worth, and he tells you 22¢. You can't believe it. Your call is at-the-money again, you paid 34¢ for it two months ago when it was at-the-money, and yet now it's only worth 22¢. What's going on?

Two things. Firstly, time decay is eating into the premium. You are now trading in the last four weeks of the option's life, and time decay is going to continue to rapidly increase during this time. If that share price isn't moving strongly, you're going to be in trouble. But the share price is going up, so why isn't your option premium screaming up with it? This is where the second thing kicks in. Remember delta? If your out-of-the-money 400 call has a delta of 0.1, it will increase by 10 per cent of the 80¢ move, or 8¢. Added onto the 14¢ premium, your option is only worth 22¢ with the move up, not even what it was worth when you bought it.

Now here's where the real trouble kicks in. Your option is at-the-money and you know the share price doesn't have to move much for your option to start increasing more rapidly in value. Rather than exit now to save some premium, you wait to see what happens. The share price does nothing over the next four weeks, and your option expires worthless.

Okay, so it just as easily could have gone up and given you a profit but that's not the point I'm trying to make here. The point is, this loss scenario could happen. So, how can you avoid allowing your option to expire worthless? How do you know when you are wrong about the market and need to exit your trade?

When you decide to buy a call, presumably your view that the share price will rise is based on some sort of financial analysis that you have undertaken. Let's say it's based on a favourable company report that you read which makes you believe the share price will rise strongly over the next three months.

The first thing you need to do is to write down your reasons for going into the trade. It's so easy to forget your reasons later on when the share price isn't doing what you expected. Not only that, but you will probably even convince yourself of some other reason—anything to allow you to stay in the market until you are proven right.

If after one month you find the share price isn't moving up, despite the favourable company report, you should ask yourself, should I still be in this market? The answer might be yes. Maybe you've undertaken some more analysis and it tells you the share price should rise from here. But once your original reason for being in the market is no longer valid, it is a huge flag that you need to think about exiting, or at least need to undertake some more analysis.

The second thing you need to do is have some sort of indicator that tells you when you are wrong in your expectations that the share price will go up. The easiest way is to base your indicator on one of the three major impacts on the premium—that is, share price, time or volatility. Ask yourself:

1. How far does the share price need to fall before I know I'm wrong about it going up?
2. When do I expect the move to happen, and therefore, when will I know I'm wrong about it going up?
3. How far does volatility have to fall before I exit my call?

A lot of traders find the use of technical indicators such as moving averages helpful for defining and refining these rules (see Chapter 14, 'Managing Your Position and Your Money', for more information on technical analysis). Just as an example of how the professional market views time decay, one very well known American fund manager has a three-day rule: if the share price doesn't do what he expects within three days, he exits the trade. While this rule obviously works for him, it is really important for you to come up with your own exit rules. Only you know your objectives, your risk-carrying ability, and your view on what the market is likely to do. (More on risk-carrying ability in Chapter 14.)

 If after all this you still don't know whether to exit your call, a good question to ask yourself is, would I buy this call option today for its current premium? If the answer is no, then you need to seriously think about why you are still in the trade.

Just because the premium defines the amount of loss at the start of a trade doesn't mean you have to risk the whole amount. In fact, it's usually the worst thing you can do, since it means you probably aren't monitoring or managing the risk in the market. The point of having exit rules is that they allow you to exit before you have given your whole premium back to the market.

So now let's look at the problem with having rules. If you have a rule that limits loss of premium by telling you to exit before you lose too much, there will be trades where you would have made more money if you had stayed in the trade. Nothing's perfect, right? The first time your exit rule knocks you out of the trade at a loss and you then see that same option returning a profit to someone else, you're going to curse me and throw away your exit rules for the next trades. The problem with this is, without rules you are completely open to the randomness in the market. This means some trades will give you profits, some will give you large losses. If your losses exceed your profits, it doesn't take a genius to work out that you will lose all your capital over time. The idea of having exit rules is to keep limiting losses so that you still have trading capital for that one time the market really runs up for you.

Clearly, if your exit rules are not working for you over time, you need to redefine them. In the meantime, stop torturing yourself by checking to see what your option is worth the day after you sell it. What does it matter? It's a bit like selling your house and then checking to see what the new owners sell it for later on. It's just bound to cause you grief.

Most call buyers lose their money because they stay in the market too long. And no wonder, since the first thing you're told is that options give you exposure over a specific period of time. You probably want to get your money's worth out of that time premium you've paid! Please, time on an option is deceptive. It doesn't work for you when you buy a call. Think of it as a hole in the bottom of a boat—at first it's not so hard to stay afloat by bucketing water from the bottom, but after a while it becomes impossible to bucket the water out as fast as it's coming in. The quicker you decide to head for shore, the better your chances of making it.

Profit Targets

If you think taking a loss on an option is difficult, you might be surprised to find that often it's harder to take a profit. Remember that unlimited reward profile? It's the number one reason why most people buy a call option—because it sounds like you can make a lot of money from one trade. And you can—that is, if you know when to take the profit. In a market which is promising unlimited rewards, it's especially difficult to know when to take it if you haven't already tried to define the potential profit at the start of the trade.

> The lure of unlimited reward is the number one reason why people lose their money when they buy a call. In the late 1980s when I was working as a commodity futures broker, sugar had a huge run-up. I had clients who bought call options, turning an investment of approximately $1,000 into $40,000 within a few weeks. And guess what? Every client gave every cent back to the market, including their original $1,000. Why? Because of greed, because of the promise of unlimited reward—why take $40,000 when this could be $50,000, $100,000, or $1,000,000? Now I know what you're thinking. You're thinking, not me, I wouldn't do that, I would take my profit and be happy with it. But statistics and experience tell me you're wrong. After all, somewhere around 80 per cent of you are going to lose all your money when you buy a call option.

So let's look at what happens to you once you buy a call and you start to make a profit.

Let's assume the same scenario as before, that you've bought your first option, an at-the-money XYZ JUN 400 call for 38¢. You know you have limited risk and unlimited profit, and that your breakeven is at $4.38. You have three months to see what's going to happen to the underlying stock and to your option. Now what?

Well, lo and behold, the underlying share price starts to rise and your option is starting to increase in value. You're starting to make that unlimited reward that your broker promised you. Your option has gone from 38¢ to 50¢ in a day. Easy money. Within the next week, the option has continued to increase in value, and is now worth $1.00. You really want to get all you can out of the market, especially since you have another two and a half months of time left. And you know you can only lose 38¢, so you have a 62¢ buffer against loss if the market should turn against you. You decide to wait to see what happens.

Another two weeks pass. XYZ shares start to fall in value; they're now trading at $4.60 and your 400 call is worth 72¢. You've lost some value, but you still have 34¢ of protection before you start losing on your trade. You feel the share price is bound to increase again within the next two months, you want to see what happens. Nothing happens for a while, and your option loses a bit more time value. Then the share price falls again—it's now at $4.00 and your call is back where it started at 38¢. You're no better or worse off than when you started, so you wait to see what happens. By expiry the share price hasn't recovered, and your option expires worthless.

Now I don't mean to sound gloomy, but this can happen very easily. How do you prevent this from happening to you?

 Firstly, do not tell yourself that unrealised profits are a buffer against loss. It is so easy to give profits back when you don't recognise them as money already earned and at risk in the market.

The profile of a bought call option tells you that when you buy an option you have limited risk, limited to the amount of premium you pay, but this is only true in a falling market. As you make profits, your risk in the market is no longer the original amount of premium— it is the new total premium amount. In the above example, the risk became $1.00. What is your potential reward at this stage? If the market has already moved substantially, it might be zero. In other words, the share price may not go any higher than it already has. You will only know this if you redefine your potential reward at the end of each day.

You must redefine your risk/reward at the end of each trading day because it changes as your option premium changes in value. Be careful as your risk increases and your potential reward decreases—it's a sure sign that you're staying in too long. Again, if you don't know whether you should exit the trade, ask yourself if you would buy a call option today with that same risk/ reward. If the answer is no, then you should seriously think about exiting your trade.

Also be careful telling yourself that you're no worse off if your option loses value and is back where it started. You *are* worse off. You have lost time value and may be entering a dangerous period of time decay on your option.

The problem with profit targets is, as with exit rules, they will sometimes take you out of the market at a lower profit than if you had none. There are ways to increase your ability to maximise profits (more about this in Chapter 14), however, apart from defining your profit potential at the start of the trade, one of the keys to being successful in trading options is to redefine the way you see price movement in the markets. Just as there is no such thing as a 'low' and 'high' price, there will never be a time when you buy at the low and sell at the high of any price movement. It's much better to think like one American fund manager who says he always takes enough out of the market to please himself, but always leaves something for someone else. If you can't think like that, then just stop yourself from looking at what your option is worth the day after you sell it. It's bound to be worth more, so stop torturing yourself!

Summary for the Bought Call Option

Action:	Purchase call, pay premium in full
Risk/reward:	Limited risk/unlimited reward
Breakeven:	Exercise price plus the premium received
View of market:	Bullish
Used for:	■ locking in a price to buy shares in the future
	■ speculating on an expected share price movement
	■ gaining short-term exposure to share price movements.

Key Rules for Trading Bought Call Options

1. Write down your reasons for buying the call option.
2. Define the reward potential before you buy the call.
3. Define profit and loss targets before you buy the call.
4. Redefine the risk/reward ratio at the close of each trading day.
5. Do not view profit as a buffer against loss.
6. Do not check the value of the call the day after you've sold it.
7. If you cannot decide whether to exit or not, ask yourself, would I buy this option today at its current premium and with its current risk/reward?

5 THE SOLD CALL

EARNING INCOME IN QUIET MARKETS

Chapter objectives:

- Define the obligations of the call seller
- Differentiate between the objectives of the buyer and those of the seller
- Discuss the effects of pricing factors on the buyer and the seller
- Construct the sold call payoff diagram
- Provide practical ways of interpreting and applying the payoff diagram
- Discuss basic entry and exit rules
- Discuss option selection based on price and time.

Before we look solely at the call seller, or writer, let's reiterate the definition of the equity call option:

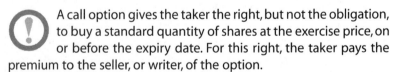 A call option gives the taker the right, but not the obligation, to buy a standard quantity of shares at the exercise price, on or before the expiry date. For this right, the taker pays the premium to the seller, or writer, of the option.

If the taker exercises his or her right to buy, the writer is required to sell a standard quantity of shares at the exercise price. For undertaking this obligation, the writer receives the premium from the taker.

Using our previous example of a BHP JAN 900 call, this tells you that:

- the taker has the right to buy 1,000 BHP shares at the exercise price of $9.00 on any day, up until the expiry date in January
- the seller, or writer, has the obligation to sell 1,000 BHP shares at $9.00 if the taker exercises his or her right.

So for every call option buyer there must be a seller. And it makes sense that if the buyer has a specific view on where the share price is going, the seller must be assuming the opposite view, since they are taking the opposite side of the contract.

In fact, options trading is what is called a 'zero-sum game'. What that means is, when one side of the contract loses money, the other side must make the exact same amount of money. Taking this a step further, what is 'good' or favourable for one side of the contract is 'bad' or unfavourable for the other side. So the risk/reward profile of one side of the call option is a mirror image of the other.

So what does this mean for the call writer? To answer that, let's look firstly at how the call writer makes a profit in the market.

Buying Low and Selling High

Hopefully by now I have convinced you that the only rule you need to know to make a profit from the market is to buy low and sell high. The good news with options is that you can sell first and still make a profit. How? By selling a high premium first and buying it back later at a lower premium. You're still 'buying low and selling high', you're just doing it in reverse.

The call writer is trying to sell a high premium, hoping the call falls in value over its life and he or she can buy it back at a lower price. So what happens to call premiums to make them fall in value?

Revisiting the Premium and the Major Pricing Factors

Remember, an option's premium comprises intrinsic value and time value. In order for the premium to fall in value, either intrinsic value or time value or both must be declining. So, let's reiterate the major pricing factors that affect the premium:

Increase In	Movement in Call Premium
Stock Price	Increase
Exercise Price	Decrease
Time to Expiry	Increase
Volatility	Increase
Dividends	Decrease
Interest Rates	Increase

What does this mean to the call writer?

- If call premiums rise when the share price rises, the writer must make a profit when the share price falls or stays flat.
- If call premiums fall due to time decay, the writer must benefit from time decay.
- If call premiums rise when volatility rises, the writer must benefit from volatility falling.
- If call premiums rise when interest rates rise, the writer must benefit from interest rates falling.

Remember that the effect of a dividend payment is factored into the call premium at the start of trading, so that if there is a dividend due on a particular stock, you will receive a lower premium for selling it in the first place. Also, the effect of interest rates is minor in the low interest rate environment at the time of writing. In addition, interest rates are usually slow to change, so their impact is often small if they do change during the life of the call option.

Summarising the Zero-Sum Game

By looking at each side of the contract, and comparing the rights and obligations, we see the following:

Call Buyer	Call Seller
Otherwise known as a taker	Otherwise known as writer or grantor
Right to exercise and buy shares	Obligation to sell shares if exercised against
Pays premium	Receives premium
View is for market to rise	View is for market to fall or stay flat
View is for volatility to stay the same or rise	View is for volatility to stay the same or fall
Time decay hurts	Time decay benefits

Three Ways to Exit

When you sell a call option, there are three things that can happen:

1. *You can be exercised against and therefore have to sell the underlying shares*

As the call writer, you do not have to have ownership of the shares at the time you write the call. There are two types of call writers: those who have ownership of the underlying shares (covered writers) and those who do not (naked writers). It is important to know that the risk profile is very different for each type of writer. For example, if you are a covered writer, you simply deliver the shares to the buyer at the time of exercise. The profit on the trade depends solely on the relationship between the original purchase price of the shares and their selling price (plus the income earned through receipt of the premium). On the other hand, if you are a naked writer at the time you are exercised against, you must go to the market and buy the shares at the current market price in order to deliver them to the buyer. The buying price of the shares at this time is logically going to be higher than the exercise price (the price at which you have the obligation to sell). So you can see the result of the trade is quite different. In this chapter we'll look solely at the naked call writer; the covered writer will be discussed in the next chapter.

Now it's fair to say that as the writer of the call, you generally want to avoid exercise. Apart from the fact that it means you're going to take a loss on the trade, there is also a high cost to exercise in terms of commissions and other fees on the share transaction. So if it is the call buyer who has the right to exercise, and this right can be exercised on any day up to and including the expiry day, how do you know when you are likely to get exercised against?

As a writer, you can get exercised at any time. However, you are more likely to get exercised when there is little or no time value left on the option. In other words, you are more likely to get exercised close to expiry. You are also likely to get exercised when the call is deep in-the-money. This doesn't mean you can't get exercised earlier or when the call is out-of-the-money—it's just less likely. As a rule of thumb, you should start to get nervous when the share price rises above your exercise price (more on this later). In addition, virtually all call options that are at-the-money will get exercised close to expiry.

Why are virtually all at-the-money calls exercised at expiry? Any professional 'market makers' who are holding at-the-money calls will exercise to buy the shares, hoping for a small movement in the share price to return them a quick profit. They can do this because they don't pay commissions, and their Exchange fees are lower than the ones you and I pay. (More on market makers in Chapter 11, 'Making Markets'.)

Now you might remember that due to the process of novation (discussed in Chapter 2), there is no direct link between any buyer and seller. So if a buyer decides to exercise, who is going to sell the shares to them?

> When a call buyer exercises the right to buy shares, one or more call writers are randomly selected to make delivery of the shares. The Exchange simply runs a computer-generated selection process which selects one or more sellers of the same option series.

Since each option is registered separately by the Exchange, if the call buyer has exercised 50 calls, anywhere from 1 to 50 separate call sellers may be selected. In other words, the Exchange does not need to look for a seller who sold 50 calls. So, if you *were* the seller of a 50 lot, you might find yourself exercised against anywhere from 1 to 50 options. It just depends on the luck of the draw.

2. You can close out your position by buying the option back before expiry (or before you are exercised against)

If the share price is falling or staying flat and your call premium is worth less than when you sold it, you can close out your position by placing an order to buy it back. Your profit will be the difference between the selling price and the buying price of the call (less any cost of trading).

> When you place your order to buy with your broker, it is important to tell him or her that it is an order to close out, or liquidate, your sold position. In this way, you ensure that the two orders cancel each other out, and you won't end up holding 'back-to-back' contracts (that is, one sold and one bought) in your portfolio. While the dollar value in the portfolio stays the same no matter what the underlying share price does in this instance, the danger with back-to-back contracts is that your chance of being exercised against is still very real.

Obviously if your call has increased in value you can still buy back the option and close out your position, but it will be at a loss. This might be appropriate to limit losses in your trading. (More about this later.)

Bear in mind that you can only liquidate your sold position if you haven't been exercised against. In other words, once you have been exercised against, there's nothing you can do but deliver the shares to the call buyer.

3. The call can expire worthless

Unlike the call buyer, who loses all his or her money if the call expires worthless, for the call seller this is an optimum result. It means that you have maximised your profit and do not need to pay another commission to your broker for closing out the position. The option simply 'disappears', and you keep all the premium.

Now that I have you geared up for allowing your option to expire worthless, be aware that you are almost always better off closing the position before expiry. In terms of risk, there only needs to be a small change in share price or volatility to turn a worthless option into one with intrinsic value at expiry. Remember those worthless gold options 10 minutes before expiry (p. 47)? While it is tempting to wait for those few extra cents of premium and avoid paying that one extra commission to your broker, an example later in the chapter will explain the real risk of this.

The Earning of Income

Okay, so by now you know that as the naked call writer:

- you earn the premium for undertaking the obligation to sell shares to the buyer if he/she exercises the right
- you aim to sell a high premium first, then to buy the call back at a lower price
- you make a profit if the share price stays steady or falls over the life of your option
- you like it if volatility is relatively high when you sell the call, because it means your premium will also be relatively high. You like it even better if volatility falls once you have sold the call because the premium will fall with it, making it even cheaper to buy back later on.

Clearly, the naked call writer has the specific view that the share price will stay flat or will fall over the life of the call option. But rather than sit on the sidelines during this flat period, the call writer takes advantage of this quiet time by earning income through the receipt of the premium. In other words, as the writer, you speculate on your market view, never intending to transact through the physical sharemarket but simply intending to make a profit on trading the option itself.

So if you earn the premium as your reward, what is the risk on the other side of your sold call?

The Option Payoff—Profit and Loss Profile for the Sold Call

Remember, a profit and loss profile is a snapshot at expiry of your particular option. It shows whether you will make a profit or loss on the trade (not including commissions and other costs of trading) according to where the share price is at expiry, and in relation to the exercise price and premium paid for your specific option. Since you already know that options are a zero-sum game and the risk/reward profile of the sold call is a mirror image of the bought call, you could probably guess that the profile is simply the reverse of the profile for the call buyer. That is, where the bought call makes a profit, you would see a loss for the call writer, and where the call buyer makes a loss, you would see a profit for the call writer.

For example, using the same illustration as before, but assuming you sell one ABC MAR 400 call for 50¢ while ABC shares are trading at $4.00, the following calculations would show:

Share Price at Expiry	Intrinsic Value	Premium	Profit/Loss
$3.00	Nil	$0.50	$0.50 profit
$3.50	Nil	$0.50	$0.50 profit
$4.00	Nil	$0.50	$0.50 profit
$4.50	$0.50	$0.50	Nil
$5.00	$1.00	$0.50	$0.50 loss
$6.00	$2.00	$0.50	$1.50 loss

Plotting the various profits and losses and then joining the dots would result in the profile opposite (Figure 5.1).

Figure 5.1
The Written Call—ABC MAR 400 Call Sold for 50¢

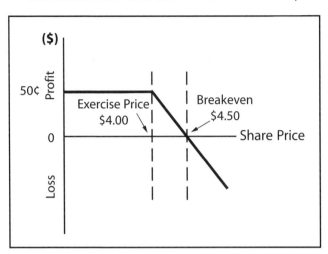

The profile for the sold call shows three really important things:

1. As the seller of a call option, you can never make more than the premium you receive for selling the option

You can see from the above profile that no matter how far the share price falls, your profit is capped at 50¢. Even if the share price falls to zero by expiry, the only profit you would make would be the premium. So it's just like selling anything, whether it's a house or a car or a call option—the only amount you can make is the amount you sell it for on the day. And it makes sense according to the zero-sum game—if the buyer can only lose 50¢, then the seller can only make 50¢. So the sold call has limited profit potential, limited to the amount of premium received for it.

2. The breakeven on the trade is at the exercise price plus the premium received

In other words, as the share price rises above the exercise price, the value of your premium starts to increase through the rise in intrinsic value. As the writer, you start to make a loss. However, you have received the premium of 50¢, and this gives you a bit of a buffer before you start making an *actual* loss. It makes sense according to the zero-sum game that this breakeven is the same for buyer and seller, since neither makes a profit nor a loss at this point.

3. As the share price rises above the breakeven, you have the potential for an unlimited loss

You can see from Figure 5.1 that once the share price rises above the breakeven point, you make a larger and larger loss as the share price continues to rise. If, for example, the share price were at $1,000 at expiry and you were forced to close the position at that time, you would make a loss of $995.50. Of course, the reality is that more than likely you would have been exercised well before this time, but you can see the potential for taking an unlimited, or at least large, loss when you sell the naked call.

The profit and loss diagram is a good way of seeing at a glance the potential profit and loss for your particular option. More importantly, it gives you a clear picture of the second aspect of risk: the probability of making that profit or loss. So let's look at how this affects the call writer.

The Reality of Unlimited Loss

The writer of a naked call has limited profit and unlimited loss potential. In terms of risk/reward that just sounds awful, doesn't it? I mean, who in their right minds would ever take on a risk/reward like that? What does it sound like to you, the possibility of making a tiny amount of money, accompanied by a huge amount of risk? Not very smart, I bet.

Before you stop reading any further and I completely talk you out of selling naked calls, let's look at the reality of that risk/reward scenario. You might recall that in the previous chapter I discussed the idea that the unlimited reward for the call buyer wasn't really unlimited, but rather undefined at the start of the trade. Well guess what? That has to mean, in terms of the zero-sum game, that the call writer doesn't have unlimited loss potential either, but rather an undefined loss potential at the start of the trade.

The loss potential for the written call is limited by two things: time and volatility. In other words, the amount the share price can rise is limited by the time remaining on the option and by the amount it generally moves around. So, it is really important to define the potential for loss on the option by reviewing potential volatility in the underlying shares.

If nothing else, it will put into perspective the terror of the concept of unlimited loss for you, so that you don't immediately discount the idea of selling naked calls.

Think about it—if somewhere around 80 per cent of call option buyers are losing their money, who's making that money? The statistics are telling us that potentially, call sellers have the ability to make repeated small profits in the market. And that makes sense, since the call seller can make a profit in two out of the three possible directions the market can go—that is, a profit can be made in flat or falling markets—while the call buyer can only make a profit in a rising market.

This is why the professional market—the fund managers, etc.—are generally sellers and not buyers. Why should they pay premium upfront when they can earn premium income and increase their returns instead? Putting the likely loss potential into perspective means that you have a more realistic risk/reward scenario and are more likely to find trades that suit your risk-carrying ability. For more on risk, see Chapter 6 and Chapter 14, which discuss ways to reduce or eliminate the unlimited risk profile of the written call by obtaining underlying share ownership or assuming other protective measures.

Defining the loss potential is also critical in regard to setting loss targets. Let's look at this in more detail.

Where to Take an Unlimited Loss

Okay, so you know that if you buy a call you have limited risk. You can relax. You think that even if you go away on holiday and forget about your position, the worst-case scenario is you lose the whole amount of premium. Not like selling a call—if you forget about that one you could lose your whole house, or worse.

I've already mentioned that the number one reason why call buyers lose their premium is this casual attitude to setting loss targets and monitoring their positions. The idea of limited risk often in fact makes call buyers place no limits on their trading. They allow natural market forces to 'limit' their losses by simply taking them out of the market at the full loss of their premium. The good news is, as a seller, you know you cannot afford to do this. There is no point in time when the market will limit your losses; you have to do it yourself. So how do you decide when this is going to be?

One way to do it is by defining the potential loss on your option using historical volatility. As the seller of the call, your expectation is for volatility to fall in the future. But what if it doesn't? What is the worst-case scenario for your option? Well, let's say you're writing a three-month option. Looking at the previous three months' historical volatility measure, you can estimate how far the share price is likely to rise over the life of your option, and therefore you can estimate the value of the call at expiry. This tells you an approximate worst-case scenario which can be likened to the loss limitation of the bought call. It doesn't mean you should allow yourself to lose this amount; in fact, it is simply the starting point for designing your exit rules.

> By defining your potential loss on the written call, you can see whether you have the risk-carrying ability to write that particular option. It is also vital in terms of money and risk management that you know how much your collective potential risk is in the market at any point in time. If you don't define it, you run the danger of ignoring the risk for the written position, and therefore underestimating your collective risk within your portfolio. (For more on risk and money management see Chapter 14.)

The good news is, the same rules apply for the call writer as for the call buyer:

- Write down your reasons for going into the trade.
- Ask yourself how far the share price has to rise before you know you're wrong about it going down or staying flat.
- Ask yourself when you think the move is going to happen.
- Ask yourself how far volatility has to rise before you know you're wrong about it falling.

> As a general rule of thumb, you should start thinking about exiting the trade once your exercise price is breached, and then become even more concerned when your breakeven point is breached. Bear in mind that your view on the share price and on volatility is for each to fall or be flat over the period of your option, so if this isn't happening, you should ask yourself if you should still be in that trade. Not only does it mean an increasing loss potential as either rises, but it also means you have another unseen risk: exercise.

Avoiding Exercise—the Breakeven and Volatility

Okay, so now you know that the risk of selling a call is theoretically unlimited, and in reality could be very large. The higher the share price rises above your breakeven point, the more it's going to cost you to close the option out, and the bigger your loss is going to be. So the breakeven point indicates how high the share price can go before you start making a loss. It is also the first point at which you will probably get really worried about exercise, because the breakeven shows you the total amount of money you will receive through the exercise of the option and the resulting share transaction. In other words, using the figures of the sold call in Figure 5.1, if the share price rises above $4.50 and you are exercised against, your loss is going to be the difference between the price you pay for the shares in the market and the $4.50 you receive in total for selling the shares. In contrast, if you are exercised against before the breakeven, you know you won't make a loss.

Reviewing volatility together with the breakeven point is a useful way of deciding which option series to sell—that is, whether to buy in-, at- or out-of-the-money. Once you know the breakeven for selling a call is at the exercise price plus the premium, you can calculate the breakevens for several different exercise prices. Using historical volatility measures over the same period will then tell you whether the share price is likely to rise above each breakeven, and therefore which exercise price you might choose in order to avoid exercise.

For example, let's say you are reviewing XYZ shares, which are currently trading at $4.00, and you are trying to decide which of the following three options to sell:

```
XYZ MAR 350   @   72¢
XYZ MAR 400   @   38¢
XYZ MAR 450   @   16¢
```

While the 350 in-the-money is tempting because of the high premium, it carries with it an immediate risk of exercise. Since your view on XYZ is for it to stay flat over the next few weeks, you quite like the look of the 400 at-the-money. With a breakeven of $4.38, you have a small amount of protection against a price rise before you start worrying about exercise, and the 38¢ of time value is more attractive than the 16¢ premium from the out-of-the-money. In addition, historical volatility for the previous six weeks was 5 per cent, so if the share price does rise, it's likely it will go no higher than $4.20, well below your breakeven. You therefore decide to sell the 400 at-the-money for 38¢, confident that you will probably avoid exercise. But the next day, you're exercised against. What happened?

 Most call sellers build in a false sense of security by not worrying about exercise prior to their breakeven point being breached. It is really important for you to distinguish between the breakeven on the trade and your chance of exercise. Remember, from day one of the option's life it is being bought and sold for differing amounts of premium: so each buyer and seller has his or her own personal breakeven point. And since a seller is randomly selected when a buyer exercises an option, you could be exercised against by a buyer with a low breakeven well before your breakeven is reached.

An example will demonstrate this. Let's say the following XYZ MAR 400 calls have been traded for the following premiums since day one:

Buyer and seller one	@	2¢	Breakeven $4.02
Buyer and seller two	@	10¢	Breakeven $4.10
Buyer and seller three	@	23¢	Breakeven $4.23
Buyer and seller four	@	38¢	Breakeven $4.38

Let's assume you are seller four, selling the call for 38¢ and with a breakeven of $4.38. Let's also assume that the share price rises to $4.10 by the next day. Buyer one, with a breakeven of $4.02, decides to exercise her right to buy the shares. With random allocation to a seller, guess who is selected to fulfil the obligation to deliver the shares? You, seller four—even though your breakeven wasn't reached.

You're probably thinking it's not so bad, since clearly you won't take a loss on the trade. However, the reality is that there is a high transaction cost to being exercised against. By the time you've paid your broker commission on buying and selling the shares and any other transaction fees that are due, you might just find that your breakeven isn't looking so good.

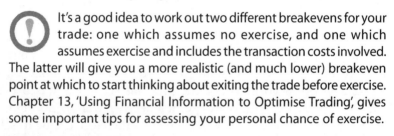 It's a good idea to work out two different breakevens for your trade: one which assumes no exercise, and one which assumes exercise and includes the transaction costs involved. The latter will give you a more realistic (and much lower) breakeven point at which to start thinking about exiting the trade before exercise. Chapter 13, 'Using Financial Information to Optimise Trading', gives some important tips for assessing your personal chance of exercise.

Defining Profit Targets

You're probably wondering why I'm going to talk about setting profit targets, when obviously the profit target is already set by the amount of premium you receive at the start of the trade. The problem is, you don't realise that profit until you place a closing trade to liquidate your position. And there's nothing more seductive than seeing that premium being credited to your account. I can guarantee that once that goes in, your whole plan will be to hang onto every cent of it. How can you do that? By waiting until expiry for it to expire worthless, when you don't even have to place a closing trade to realise the maximum profit.

I already mentioned earlier that one of the worst things you can do, whether as a buyer or a writer, is to stay in until expiry. Expiry is usually the most volatile of all times, when professional traders are moving between the physical shares, equity options, equity futures and other derivatives products in order to square their books and try to make a last-ditch profit. This means that share prices, and therefore option prices, can really move around close to expiry. You might just find your at-the-money or even out-of-the-money calls expire in-the-money.

But surely, I hear you ask, a call which is almost worthless near expiry has little chance of expiring in-the-money? Surely waiting until expiry carries low risk? Well, let's look at what that risk can be.

Let's say you have written an ABC JUN 400 call for 50¢, it is two days before expiry, XYZ is trading at $4.00 and your call is worth 2¢. The question is, what is your potential profit at this point in time? Most people answer '48¢', but the right answer is 2¢—after all, you have already made 48¢ on the trade, since all you have to do is close the position to realise the 48¢ profit. Your potential profit, in other words, the profit you could make in the future, is 2¢. By staying in the trade, all you are waiting for is another 2¢ profit. And why not, you ask, since there's only two days to go, and if you do nothing and the option expires worthless, you make a further 2¢ and don't have to pay another commission for closing the position. What's the risk in that?

Let's examine it. At the start of the trade your risk was unlimited, or at least potentially large, and your reward was 50¢. At two days before expiry, unless you have done something to offset that unlimited risk, it still exists. So, if you were to redefine your risk/reward scenario at that time, it would show that you have unlimited risk for a potential 2¢ reward. Sound good to you? Hopefully you answered no, and if you did, in this situation you should be asking yourself if you should still be in this trade. Again, if you cannot answer that, ask yourself if you would go into the market today selling another call for 2¢.

Remember to redefine your risk/reward scenario at the close of business each day. It's a really easy way to see whether you should still be in the trade. Be careful if you see your risk increasing and your reward diminishing—it should make you think about exiting the market.

Bear in mind that the decision to liquidate the position might come sooner than two days before expiry. For example, if the option premium were to fall to 12¢ within a few days of selling the option you might decide to exit then; you might even exit if it were trading at 23¢. Don't be greedy or insist on realising the whole sold premium. Your number one priority should always be reducing risk, and increasing returns should come firmly second.

> Remember, the quicker you realise your profit, the higher your return is when it is annualised. Not only that, but it means you have freed trading capital for another trade which might return you another 27¢ to 50¢, rather than hanging on for only a few cents of leftover premium.

While you might think that the risk in the above example is small, it reminds me of a story a broker told me once. He had a client who was used to writing large volumes of calls over various stocks. On one occasion, his client sold a 50 lot of calls for 45¢ each and two days before expiry the calls were trading at 2¢. His broker suggested he close his position but the client, obviously consulting his crystal ball, declared, "Why should I? In two days' time the calls will expire worthless. I'll make another 2¢ per call, and I won't have to pay you a 50 lot of commission for the closing sale." Unfortunately, the client's crystal ball was obviously broken, because at expiry the stock shot up in price and the calls were suddenly worth 90¢ each. Instead of making a nice profit of $21,500 (43¢ per share × 1,000 shares × 50 lot), he lost something in the order of $22,500 (45¢ per share × 1,000 shares × 50 lot)—all because he was greedy for an extra 2¢ per share, or $1,000 more. You wouldn't do that, of course, would you?

> Rather than thinking of the premium you receive as money already guaranteed and earned, think of the premium as potential profit. That's exactly what it is, since you don't receive the profit (as opposed to the premium) until you close your position. This should help you monitor and manage the profit, relative to the potential for large loss.

Which Option to Sell—the Direct Risk/Reward Relationship

When looking at which option series to sell, the general rule of thumb is you maximise your gain selling at-the-money options when you are neutral in your outlook. In other words, the theory is that if the share price stays completely flat until the expiry of the option, you gain the most time premium for selling the at-the-money call, since it has the most time premium of all the series. If you are slightly bullish, on the other hand, you might decide to sell the out-of-the-money call, since the share price can rise slightly before you start worrying about exercise. If you are slightly bearish on the underlying shares you might decide to write the in-the-money—by doing this you get a high premium, and if you are right about the share price falling quickly, you might avoid exercise.

Again, this relationship between the maximisation of your profit and the exercise price is shown in profit and loss profiles. The exercise price is the point of maximisation of your profit, since any option which is at-the-money at expiry will expire worthless, enabling the writer to keep the whole premium. Unfortunately, what the profit and loss profile doesn't show is the risk of exercise on the position at that point or during the life of the option. In other words, while the theory says the at-the-money call maximises your gain when you are neutral, you already know that once you write the at-the-money, it is possible to get exercised against almost straight away. And the at-the-money will almost certainly be exercised at expiry.

I think writing in-the-money calls is also fraught with danger unless you have underlying ownership of the shares. I don't know of any brokers who would recommend this to a client without also recommending that it be a covered call, since the risk of exercise is so high immediately. The only option which is going to give you peace of mind against exercise is the out-of-the-money—but look at how tiny the premium is for writing it.

There is a direct relationship between the reward you receive via the premium and the risk of exercise. The higher the premium you receive for writing the call, the higher your risk of exercise. Always be aware that while you might be planning to write a high premium in order to buy it back and close it out later, there is another party to your transaction and a hidden risk—exercise by the buyer. So it might be better to forgo some premium to avoid the high cost of exercise and give you some peace of mind.

Which Option to Sell—the Perils of Time

Okay, so now you have decided on which exercise price to sell, knowing that the higher the premium you receive the more risk you take on. There's one more selection criterion that you have to decide on—which expiry month?

Just as for the bought call, the expiry month you select will depend on:

- your view of the market. How long you expect the share price to remain flat or when you think it will fall—the next few days, the next few weeks, months?
- how liquid the different expiry months are
- time decay.

Remember that the most liquid months are the spot month and three-month options, and liquidity affects both the buyer and the seller, since it means that pricing is more efficient in these options. Always trade in the more liquid expiry months, otherwise you'll receive less for writing the call and will have to pay more to close it out.

The other consideration is time decay. If time decay benefits the writer, when is the best time to write a call option?

The best time to write a call is when time decay is rapidly increasing in the last four to six weeks of an option's life. So while the call buyer should generally avoid this period, it is the optimum time for the call writer. It means that without anything else happening, just because of the passage of time the call will naturally and aggressively lose value.

Be careful writing calls when there is a lot of time before expiry. While the extra time premium might be attractive, remember that receiving a higher premium means taking on a higher risk. The longer you have until expiry, the more chances the share price has to move against you. Options are meant to be used as short-term trading instruments—be prepared to trade your positions over only a few weeks or even days to optimise your returns.

Most sellers take a loss because they stay in the market too long. Just like the buyers, on the one hand they refuse to accept they are wrong about the market direction and therefore refuse to take a small loss, and on the other hand they are slow to take a modest, but highly leveraged, profit.

One of the other mistakes sellers make is not to understand their risk in the market, or their obligation to meet that risk. It is essential for every seller to have a good understanding of the way the Exchange monitors and manages this risk for you through the process of margining. You might like to look next at Chapter 12, 'Managing Risk—Your Margin for Error', which explains the process in detail. Otherwise, stay with me and we'll look at the covered writer.

Summary for the Naked Sold Call Option

Action:	Sell call, receive premium in full
Risk/Reward:	Limited reward/unlimited risk
Breakeven:	Exercise price plus the premium received
View of Market:	Neutral to slightly bearish
Used for:	▪ earning income in quiet markets
	▪ speculating on an expected share price movement.

Key Rules for Trading Sold Call Options

1. Write down your reasons for selling the call option.
2. Define the unlimited loss potential before you sell the call.
3. Define profit and loss targets before you sell the call.
4. Redefine the risk/reward ratio at the close of each trading day.
5. Do not check the value of the call the day after you've liquidated it.
6. If you cannot decide whether to exit or not, ask yourself, would I sell this option today at its current premium and with its current risk/reward?

6 THE BUY WRITE

A SHARE TRADER'S BREAD AND BUTTER

Chapter objectives:

- Define the buy write
- Differentiate between the naked writer and the buy writer
- Discuss option selection based on price and time
- Construct the buy write payoff diagram
- Provide practical ways of interpreting and applying the payoff diagram
- Explain the relationship between return and protection elements
- Discuss basic entry and exit rules.

So far you know that:

- The call writer has the obligation to deliver shares if he or she is exercised against.
- For undertaking the obligation, the writer receives the premium.
- The writer is still looking to buy low and sell high, but in reverse—that is, sell a high premium initially and then buy the call back for a lower premium later on.
- The writer takes advantage of time decay on the option, and so anticipates a flat or falling market.
- The writer generally wants to avoid exercise, due to the high transaction costs involved in the delivery process.

You might also recall that for the naked writer, the loss potential is unlimited. And even though I probably convinced you that it is not really unlimited (or at least lessened your fear of it), it might still sound like a rather large risk to adopt. And it can be. That's why the majority of call writers are covered writers. Somewhere around 95 per cent of call writers in the Australian market have underlying ownership of the shares. This is certainly true of the professional fund managers—as holders of large numbers of shares, it makes sense that they use their large investment to increase their returns by earning premium income for writing calls over the shares they hold.

Twice as Nice

Okay, so you're a holder of large parcels of shares. Maybe these shares give you capital gains over a period of time if you hold them long enough. Maybe some even give you a decent yield via dividend income during the year. But there is a way to make your shares work harder for you, and that's by increasing your yield by writing calls over the stock you hold.

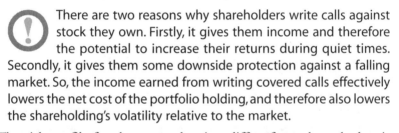 There are two reasons why shareholders write calls against stock they own. Firstly, it gives them income and therefore the potential to increase their returns during quiet times. Secondly, it gives them some downside protection against a falling market. So, the income earned from writing covered calls effectively lowers the net cost of the portfolio holding, and therefore also lowers the shareholding's volatility relative to the market.

The risk profile for the covered writer differs from the naked writer because of the underlying share ownership. As I mentioned before, if you are exercised against as a covered writer, you simply deliver the shares that you already own. The profit you make on the trade is the difference between the original price you paid for the shares and the selling price through exercise, plus the premium income you've earned.

 In other words, if the call is established correctly, the covered writer has a known profit on exercise. As long as you're happy with the return you'll receive, the covered write is a relatively low-risk way of enhancing your returns.

The Buy Write versus the Covered Write

So how does a buy write differ from a covered write? There's not much difference, since the view of the market is the same and the result is the same. However, while the covered writer already has underlying share ownership, the buy writer enters the sharemarket to buy shares at the same as writing the call option.

So a strict textbook definition would be as follows:

 The buy write is the simultaneous writing of a call and the purchase of the same number of shares underlying the option.

It is important to stress that the share ownership must be of the same number of shares underlying the option. While this is usually 1,000 shares per one option, it can be different if there has been a bonus or rights issue during the life of the option. It is important as the buy writer that you know how many shares are underlying the particular option, so that you buy the exact amount.

The next question is, why would you buy shares and immediately write a call option against them?

Buying and Writing

 Generally, the buy writer has a long-term view that the shares will increase in value and a short-term view that the share price will stay relatively flat. Rather than waiting to enter the market later when the shares show some sign of bullishness, buy writers aim to lower their buying price of the shares through the receipt of the premium. If they are right, and the share price remains flat over the life of the option, they keep the premium to offset the buying price. If the share price falls slightly, the premium income also offsets that decline. And if the share price rises strongly and they are exercised against, they are prepared to sell their shares at an acceptably high return, foregoing the extra capital appreciation should the shares continue to rise strongly.

For example, let's say you've been looking at XYZ shares, which are currently trading at $6.00. You quite like the look of XYZ as a long-term hold, but are concerned about a flat market in the short-term. You don't really want to pay $6,000 for 1,000 shares if they're not going to perform over the next six weeks, but would be happy to hold them over that period if you could buy them at a discount. You decide to buy the 1,000 XYZ shares and at the same time sell a six-week call option. So you're happy to hold the shares at a discount if the market stays quiet or, alternatively, to earn a quick high return through exercise should XYZ show unexpected signs of bullishness.

The following example shows you what to do:

Buy 1,000 XYZ shares	@	$6.00 per share	= $6,000
Sell 1 × XYZ JUN 600 call	@	$0.25	= $250
Actual buying price of shares			= $5,750

Since the total buying price of the shares is reduced by the premium, you effectively receive a discount on buying of around 4 per cent in our example. And what does this discount represent? The amount the share price can fall before you start showing a loss. Thus, you receive some downside protection via the premium when you sell the call against the shares.

Let's look at what you have so far:

- You have ownership of 1,000 XYZ shares.
- You have effectively bought the shares for $5.75 per share.
- You have an obligation to sell those 1,000 XYZ shares for $6.00 on exercise.
- The obligation exists for the next six weeks, until expiry of the option.

Figure 6.1, below, shows the relationship between your effective buying price of the shares and your selling price should you be exercised against. It also shows you where your risk is if the market falls, or alternatively, if it shows unexpected signs of bullishness above your exercise price (discussed below).

Figure 6.1
XYZ Buy Write

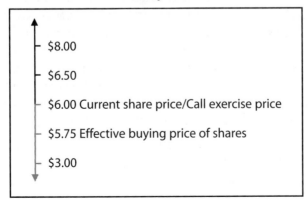

What can happen in the next six weeks? Remember, there are only three things that might happen to the share price over the life of the option: it can go up, it can go down, or it can stay completely flat. Let's look at what happens in our example for each of these three scenarios.

1. XYZ shares fall in price

If XYZ shares fall in price, you have 25¢ of protection via the premium before you start taking a loss. Unfortunately, should XYZ continue to fall beyond $5.75, you will be losing on a one-for-one basis—but that's always the risk when you buy shares. Fortunately, the risk is lessened, together with your overall loss, since your effective buying price was lower than if you had not sold the call. Should XYZ fall to $3.00, for example, your loss on the buy write would be $2.75, as opposed to $3.00 had you not sold the call.

2. XYZ shares stay flat

If XYZ shares are at exactly $6.00 by expiry of the call, the call will expire worthless. As the call writer, you keep all of the 25¢ of premium. Now, you might be disappointed since your shares have not gone up in value, but by keeping the premium you have at least earned a return over the period. Had you not written the call and simply bought the shares, you would show no return.

3. XYZ shares rise in value

Should XYZ shares rise in value, let's say to $6.50, you might be exercised against. If this happens, you will have to sell your XYZ shares at $6.00 per share. Since your effective buying price of the shares was $5.75, you make a 25¢ profit.

This is where it gets interesting. What is your total profit should the share price rise to $8.00 and you are exercised against? Hopefully you've answered 25¢, because you've locked in the selling price of the shares (i.e. the exercise price) at $6.00, and with your effective buying price of $5.75 that means you have a 25¢ profit. Even if the share price rises to $100 and you're exercised against, it still means you have a 25¢ profit. In other words, you will never earn more than 25¢ no matter how high the share price rises.

 It is important to understand that the buy writer locks in the selling price of the shares via the exercise price of the call, and therefore also locks in the maximum profit that can be made on the trade. Because of this, one of the major risks is an unexpected strong rise in the share price, because it means the buy writer forgoes the extra capital appreciation on the shares. On the other hand, with limited downside protection via the premium, the second major risk is an unexpected fall in the share price—always the case when you buy shares.

Damage Control

Just like the naked writer, the buy writer generally wants to avoid exercise. And the beauty of options is that they are flexible—just because you have written the call as part of a buy write doesn't mean you have to keep it if the market is moving against you! If the share price were rising strongly above your exercise price, you might decide to liquidate the sold call in order to avoid exercise. You may want to hold onto the shares and let them fully appreciate in value, rather than lose them at a fixed return.

You might remember that in order to avoid exercise, the general rule of thumb is you should start to get nervous as soon as your exercise price is hit. After all, your analysis prior to entering the trade suggested this wouldn't happen, otherwise you wouldn't have chosen that particular exercise price, would you? So in the above example, you would get nervous as soon as the share price showed any signs of bullishness. And certainly, you wouldn't sit back and do nothing should you believe the share price was going to rise to $8.00. If you didn't want to lose the shares, it would be better to buy back the sold call prior to being exercised against.

Bear in mind that if you decide to liquidate your call in a strongly rising market, you will have to pay more for it than the original premium you received. In other words, you will take a loss on the call. However, the loss on the call won't be as large as the profit you'll be making on the shares as they increase in value. Why not? Because of the call's delta. As long as you are quick to exit the call, and its delta is less than 1, your shares, with a delta of 1, will be increasing at a faster rate. It might be better to suffer a small loss on the call if you believe the shares are going to rise high enough to make it worth your while.

The Option Payoff—Profit and Loss Profile for the Buy Write

You've already seen the profit and loss profile for the naked call writer, and you might be tempted to think that the profile for the buy writer is the same. You're still writing a call, aren't you? However, remember that the risks of the two trades are different. While the naked writer has potentially unlimited loss, the buy writer, through ownership of the shares, does not. In addition, the naked writer is only concerned about the change in option premium, not the change in the share price relative to any shareholding. So if the risks or the rewards aren't the same for each transaction, the profiles cannot be the same.

In order to plot the profile for the buy write, it is necessary to take into account the profit or loss made on the share transaction as well as the option leg. Using the example of buying 1,000 XYZ shares at $6.00 per share and selling 1 × XYZ JUN 600 call at 25¢, the following calculations can be made:

Share Price at Expiry	Stock Profit/Loss	Call Profit/Loss	Total Profit/Loss
$5.00	$1.00 loss	$0.25 profit	$0.75 loss
$5.50	$0.50 loss	$0.25 profit	$0.25 loss
$5.75	$0.25 loss	$0.25 profit	Nil
$6.00	Nil	$0.25 profit	$0.25 profit
$6.50	$0.50 profit	$0.25 loss	$0.25 profit
$7.00	$1.00 profit	$0.75 loss	$0.25 profit

Plotting the various profits and losses and then joining them would result in the following profile:

Figure 6.2
The Buy Write—Buy 1,000 XYZ shares at $6.00,
Sell XYZ JUN 600 Call at $0.25

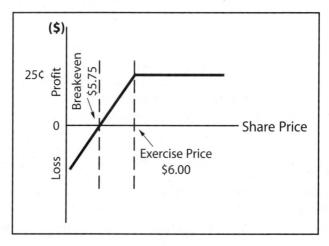

The profile for the buy write shows three really important things:

1. **As the buy writer, your maximum profit is the difference between the buying price of the stock and the selling price through exercise, plus the premium received**

In other words:

> Maximum profit = call exercise price – stock purchase price + premium

You can see from the profile that buy writers maximise their profit at expiry if the share price is at the exercise price of the call. In other words, even if the share price rises above the exercise price, the buy writer will never earn more than the predetermined profit.

2. **The breakeven is at the purchase price of the shares, minus the premium received**

Again, since the effective buying price is reduced by the premium received, the share price has some downside protection before you start taking a loss.

3. **As the share price falls below the breakeven, you have the potential to make large losses**

Clearly, this is always the case when you buy shares. And just like any share buyer, the loss potential for the buy writer is not unlimited since the share price cannot fall further than zero. In actual fact, the loss potential is limited and completely defined—the maximum loss is the effective buying price of the shares, or the breakeven on the profile. In other words, in the above example, the maximum loss potential is $5.75 should the share price fall all the way to zero.

Contrasting the profiles for the buy writer (p. 74) and the naked writer (p. 56–57), you can see that they, in fact, make profits under different market conditions. Where the naked writer makes a profit in a flat or falling market, the buy writer makes the profit in a neutral to slightly bullish market.

Obviously the buy writer can also make a profit in a strongly bullish market, however the profit potential is capped at the exercise price of the written call. Because of this, if you are strongly bullish it might be more appropriate to instigate a strategy that wouldn't cap your profit potential—for example, by buying shares outright or by buying a call. Remember, the advantage of trading options is that they are flexible and allow you to tailor your market view. Always give yourself the best opportunity, combined with an appropriate risk, for your market view.

The Hidden Risk of Maximising Profit

All right, so you just learned from the profile that buy writers maximise their profit at-the-money at expiry. In other words, even if the share price is higher than this, they still make the same profit. But there is also a hidden risk that the profile doesn't show—your risk of exercise. Remember, at-the-money calls are usually exercised around expiry, and while this doesn't theoretically change the 25¢ return in the above example, it does in reality due to exercise transaction costs. It might, therefore, be appropriate to plan to buy the call back prior to expiry and eliminate your exercise risk. Sure, it means you'll lose a few cents to close the call, but it's the only way to ensure you keep your shares if you still want to.

Of course there's another way to reduce your chance of exercise, and that's by writing out-of-the-money calls. But I'll get a lower premium for doing it, I hear you say? You're right, but you'll also increase your profit on exercise. Let's see how.

Which Option to Sell? In-, At- and Out-of-the-Money Buy Writes

Before we consider which option to write, let's first look at what the risks are for the buy writer, and how they differ from those of the naked writer. For the naked writer, the only risk is a strongly rising market. So, the naked writer's risk increases with the rising share price—that is, the risk of unlimited or large losses becomes increasingly real, together with the risk of exercise. While buy writers don't have the same risk of unlimited loss as the share price rises, they do have the same risk of exercise. In fact, the risk of large losses actually arises for the buy writer as the share price falls. So the buy writer faces two risks: the risk of a strongly rising market (the risk of exercise) and the risk of a strongly falling market (the risk of large losses). How do you manage both of them?

As there are two major risks with the buy write, it is important for you to distinguish which is your greatest fear: the fear of some bearishness in the share price (losing money), or the fear of some bullishness (losing your shares). If your fear is for some bearishness, you would want more downside protection. Since the amount of premium you receive for writing the call equates to the amount of downside protection, you might choose a higher premium

76

to write—that is, you might write an in-the-money call. Conversely, if your fear is of some bullishness, you might write a lower premium in order to avoid exercise—that is, you might write an out-of-the-money.

Obviously, if you write an in-the-money call your risk of exercise is immediate. And how much would your profit be if you were exercised? Pretty small, since you would be selling shares at a lower price than you bought them. It's not a very smart idea unless you are quite bearish on the shares, or you had bought them previously at a much lower price than the current price (that is, rather than instigating it as a buy write, you are simply a covered writer). On the other hand, if you write the out-of-the-money your tiny premium won't give you much downside protection but your profit on exercise will be quite high, since you will be selling your shares at a much higher price than you bought them.

In other words, there is an indirect relationship between the amount of downside protection you receive via the premium and the profit you will receive on exercise. The more downside protection you have, the lower will be your profit on exercise. Conversely, the less downside protection you have, the higher will be your profit on exercise.

Let's look at an example (Figure 6.3). We're going to assume that XYZ shares are trading at $6.00, and that you do an in-, at- and out-of-the-money buy write. We're then going to assume each written call is exercised, so you can see the resulting profit on each.

Figure 6.3
In-, At- and Out-of-the-Money Buy Writes

1. In-the-money buy write:

Buy 1,000 XYZ shares	@	$6.00
Sell 1 × XYZ JUN 550 call	@	$0.62
Effective buying price		$5.38

Profit on exercise = Call exercise price − stock purchase price + premium
= $5.50 − $6.00 + $0.62
= $0.12

2. At-the-money buy write:

Buy 1,000 XYZ shares	@	$6.00
Sell 1 × XYZ JUN 600 call	@	$0.25
Effective buying price		$5.75

Profit on exercise = Call exercise price − stock purchase price + premium
= $6.00 − $6.00 + $0.25
= $0.25

(cont'd)

Figure 6.3 (cont'd)
In-, At- and Out-of-the-Money Buy Writes

3. Out-of-the-money buy write:	Buy 1,000 XYZ shares	@	$6.00
	Sell 1 × XYZ JUN 650 call	@	$0.17
	Effective buying price		$5.83

Profit on exercise = Call exercise price − stock purchase price + premium
= $6.50 − $6.00 + $0.17
= $0.67

You can see with the in-the-money the share price can fall quite far before you start taking a loss on the buy write. However, the profit on exercise is relatively small. Conversely, with the out-of-the-money call, the profit on exercise is high, but the downside protection is minimal.

One of the main reasons the buy write is so popular is that at the time of undertaking it, you can see exactly what you are getting. And even in the case of the in-the-money buy write which has a relatively small profit, you can see exactly what your profit is going to be if you are exercised. Obviously, if you don't like it, you don't do it.

Ultimately, when choosing which exercise price to write, it is important that you are happy with the return that you will receive. After all, the whole point of writing calls against stock is to increase returns, isn't it? So let's look at how you measure those returns.

The Return on Investment

Since the buy write or covered write includes stock ownership, there needs to be some way of measuring the different returns that you receive for writing different exercise prices. One of the best ways to decide between two different options is by comparing the return on investment for each.

The formula for calculating the annualised return on a buy write is:

$$\frac{\text{Time premium}}{\text{Stock price}} \times 100 \times \frac{365 \text{ (days in the year)}}{\text{Days until expiry}}$$

For example, let's say you write an at-the-money XYZ JUN 400 call for 22¢. At the time, there are 63 days left until expiry. Your calculation would look like the following:

$$\frac{0.22}{4.00} \times 100 \times \frac{365}{63} = 31.9\%$$

You can see from this formula that the buy write only takes into account the value of the time premium in the calculation. This is because you do not earn a return on any intrinsic value that you have written. And this is why writing in-the-money calls results in a lower return—there is a cost to it through intrinsic value.

Please note that the formula assumes that the stock price is unchanged at expiry of the call option, and therefore does not calculate the return if the share price is above or below this figure. In addition, it does not take into account either exercise or the return you would receive according to the purchase price of your shares. It does, however, give you a snapshot of relative returns at the time of writing, and it's pretty obvious that you might choose the call that returns a relatively higher return over another one.

Luckily, you don't have to make these calculations yourself. For more information on where to find annualised returns, you might like to read Chapter 13, 'Using Financial Information to Optimise Trading'.

Managing the Downside Risk

The writing of a call against stock you hold gives you a way of protecting your shares from minor declines in the share price. In addition, you can choose how much protection you have by selecting an in-, at- or out-of-the-money call. What can you do beyond that? Well, like any share purchase it really depends on your view of the stock, your trading personality (that is, whether you are a long-term or short-term holder), and your risk-carrying ability.

When you buy write, you must be prepared for two things: that you might lose the stock, and conversely, that you might have to hold the stock. So the general rule of thumb is, do not buy write against stock you don't want to lose, or against stock you don't want to own. With random exercise in the market, there is always the risk that you will get hit for exercise, or that you won't.

But what are the real risks of exercise for the writer?

The Real Risks of Exercise

The Exchange usually quotes that somewhere around 15 per cent of options are ever exercised. Now as a writer, you know that these statistics are extremely important, because they give you an idea of your own chance of being exercised against. But don't be misled— this is an average statistic from the last 20 or so years of trading across every series of option that ever traded. And you know what they say about statistics!

The reality is that during extreme volatility and in strongly trending markets, the exercise statistic for any single series can be extremely high. For example, I have seen times when around 40 per cent of options in a particular series or class have been exercised. But when you average it out over time, it looks like only a small percentage are exercised. Not much help to you if you're a writer during one of those strong swings. So it is important to understand that at any point of time, your chance of exercise could be lower or higher than these often-quoted statistics. If you want to know your real chance of exercise, there are some quick tips in Chapter 13, 'Using Financial Information to Optimise Trading'. If you are interested to find out more, the Exchange publishes full exercise statistics for each class of options.

So you've decided to hold those shares for long-term capital appreciation. You know you can buy write during quiet times, even earn some downside protection. But what about those expected large declines? Are you prepared to ride out all the corrections, profit-taking and major dips in the share price, and just watch your portfolio lose unrealised profits when it does? If you aren't, and would like to find a way to reduce the company and market risk in your portfolio, then stay with me, and we'll enter the world of the put option.

Summary for the Buy Write

Action: Buy shares and sell the same numbers of calls, receive premium in full

Risk/Reward: Maximum profit = call exercise price – stock purchase price + premium; Maximum loss = stock purchase price – the premium received

Breakeven: Purchase price of the shares – the premium received

View of Market: Neutral to slightly bullish

Used for: Earning income in quiet markets

---

7 THE EQUITY PUT OPTION DEFINED

Chapter objectives:

- Define an equity put option
- Reiterate the two components of premium
- Describe the effect of different pricing factors on the time premium
- Differentiate between the effect of pricing factors on calls and puts
- Provide practical ways to apply pricing theory.

By now you should be feeling pretty confident about the buying and selling of call options. Most investors find the concept of buying and then selling something fairly straightforward, and since most share investors are comfortable with the idea of buying shares, the bought call tends to be the first option trade tried by new investors. After all, it's fairly easy to understand owning the right to buy something in the future, isn't it?

But what if you had the right to sell something in the future? It might sound straightforward until I add that you don't have to own that something in order to have the right to sell it. Confused? Most people are when they enter the upside-down world of the put option. That's probably why there are somewhere around five times as many calls traded as puts. Apart from the fact that most share traders are optimists and are used to looking for buying opportunities, the put option tends to be a little harder to understand. But bear with me (no pun intended!). I promise by the end of this, the concept will be as easy to understand as that of the call.

Defining the Equity Put

Let's start with the textbook definition of a put option:

A put option gives the taker the right, but not the obligation, to sell a standard quantity of shares at the exercise price, on or before the expiry date.
If the taker exercises the right to buy, the writer is required to buy a standard quantity of shares at the exercise price.

The first thing you might notice with this definition is its similarity to the call option definition. That is, the taker again has the right, and the writer again has the obligation to do something. In the case of the bought call, it is a right to buy shares, and in the case of the bought put, it is a right to sell shares. Because it can get a little tricky to talk about buying something in order to sell something else, I find it easier to use the terms 'taker' and 'writer' instead of 'buyer' and 'seller' when I talk about puts. It just helps to keep it straight in my mind.

Be aware that while there are similarities in the rights and obligations on each side of puts and calls, they are not the opposite sides of the same transaction. They are completely different instruments that allow you to do different things. It's like the good old apples and oranges analogy. If you buy an apple you have to sell an apple to get rid of it, and if you buy an orange, you have to sell an orange to get rid of it. In the same way, if you buy a call, you have to sell a call to get rid of it, and if you buy a put, you have to sell a put to get rid of it.

An example of a put might be: BHP JAN 900 put. This tells you that:

- the taker has the right to sell 1,000 BHP shares at the exercise price of $9.00 on any day, up to and including the expiry date in January
- the writer has the obligation to buy 1,000 BHP shares at $9.00 if the taker exercises his/her right.

Now, what if BHP were trading at $7.50—wouldn't you like to have a few of these taken puts in your portfolio? Wouldn't it be great to be able to sell BHP shares for $1.50 more than everyone else in the market? Hopefully you are now starting to see the relationship between the current share price and the exercise price, and the advantage the taker has through exercise if he or she has the right to sell shares at a higher price than the current market.

The only component missing from our example is the premium. And you know that the definition says the premium is agreed to between the taker and writer. So, if you decided you wanted to take one of these put options, how much would you be willing to pay for it? Or alternatively, if you wanted to write a put option, how much premium would you need to receive for having the obligation to buy BHP at $1.50 more than the current market?

The Advantage of Selling Shares at a Higher Price than the Rest of the Market: Intrinsic Value

Before you answer these questions, let's take a step back from our BHP example. Let's say that you own 1,000 BHP shares, and your analysis predicts that there might be a rather large decline in BHP's share price over the next three months. What can you do? Well, firstly, you might try to convince yourself that since you're a long-term holder, it doesn't really matter. After all, you don't really make a loss on the shares if you continue holding them. But that's like saying you don't really take a loss on your house if property values decline—if nothing else, it's at least an opportunity cost, since the money you have tied up there could be invested somewhere else where you could make a return over the period. So what next? Do you panic-sell? What if you're wrong, and BHP continues to rise over the next three months? Wouldn't it be great to be able to lock in a high selling price for your BHP shares today, but not have to sell them if BHP rises? Wouldn't you like to have the time to see what BHP's share price does over the next three months before you make a decision to sell or hold?

With BHP trading at $7.50, you decide to take the following three put options: an 800, a 750 and a 700 put option, giving you the right, but no obligation, to sell your 1,000 BHP shares for $8.00, $7.50 or $7.00 through exercise. So your three puts look something like this:

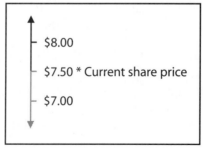

Now everyone else in the market must sell their shares for the current market price of $7.50; however, since you have taken your three put options you have a choice. You can decide to sell your shares for $8.00, $7.50 or $7.00 through exercising an option. Knowing that the first rule of successful trading in the sharemarket is 'buy low and sell high', which one would you exercise? The $8.00 put, since by exercising your right to sell BHP for $8.00, you receive 50¢ more than the rest of the market. What is this 50¢ advantage called? Intrinsic value.

> Remember, the option's intrinsic value is its *real* value. It is the advantage through exercise; the profit you receive from selling the shares through exercise of the option and then immediately buying back your shares at the current share price. When you can receive more than the current market price for your shares through exercising your put, you have intrinsic value.

Is there any intrinsic value in the BHP 750 put? Or the 700 put? The answer is no. The 800 put is the only one with real value, or profit through exercise, because it is the only option that allows you to 'sell high', i.e. higher than the current market price.

> To phrase it simply, a put option has intrinsic value when its exercise price is higher than the current share price.

It can be confusing to remember how to calculate the intrinsic value for puts and calls. The best way I have of remembering it is by remembering the fundamental investment rule of 'buy low and sell high'. Since a call option gives the taker the right to buy shares, calls have intrinsic value when you can buy low, or lower than the current share price. Conversely, since a put option gives the taker the right to sell shares, you have intrinsic value when you can sell high, or higher than the current share price.

As the share price moves lower and lower below your exercise price, the advantage through exercise increases and therefore the intrinsic value increases. This is one reason why as the share price falls, your put option premiums rise with it (all things being equal).

> You might remember that with a call option, there is a direct relationship between the share price movement and the movement of the premium. That is, when the share price rises, so do the call premiums (all things being equal). However, with the put option, there is an inverse relationship between the share price movement and the premium movement. It is when the share price

falls that the put option premium rises. See Figure 7.1 and Figure 7.2, below, for a visual representation of this.

Figure 7.1
Premium Movement of Calls and Puts when Share Price Falls

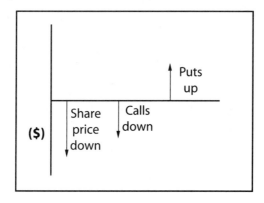

Figure 7.2
Premium Movement of Calls and Puts when Share Price Rises

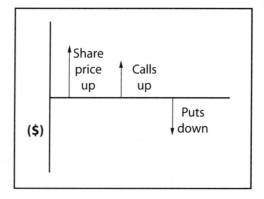

This is why you take puts in order to trade a falling market. You can buy a put for a low premium hoping that the share price falls and the premium increases, and you can sell it later for a higher premium. Still with me? Great, let's look at some more jargon.

In-, At- and Out-of-the-Money

You might recall that a call option has intrinsic value, and is therefore in-the-money, when its exercise price is below the current share price. The concept is reversed for the put option.

A put option with an exercise price above the current share price has intrinsic value and is referred to as being **in-the-money**. A put option that is at the current share price is referred to as being **at-the-money**. A put option that has an exercise price below the current share price, and therefore no advantage through exercise, is referred to as being **out-of-the-money**. See Figure 7.3, below:

Figure 7.3
Put Option Exercise Prices

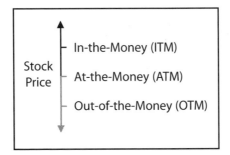

The Premium Revisited

Just when you thought that everything must be reversed for puts and calls, the good news is that the put premium still comprises intrinsic and time value. Because of this, the same rules apply, as follows:

- Time value represents the market's perception of the put's potential for profit in the future, coupled with the potential return.
- Time value is greatest for the at-the-money puts.
- The more time value there is on a put, the higher the premium will be.
- The less time value there is on a put, the lower the premium will be. That is, a put option's time value decays over its life.
- Time decay for puts is not constant. As a general rule of thumb, you will lose approximately one-third of your time value over the first half of the put's life, and two-thirds in the second half.
- In the last four to six weeks of the put's life, there is usually little, if any, time value left, unless the share price is falling rapidly.

While you can see that there are many similarities between the time value of puts and calls, there is one major difference. Put options have much less time value relative to calls. An example will demonstrate this.

Let's say we're looking at XYZ puts and calls, and we see the following options listed:

	Call Premium	Call Time Value	Put Premium	Put Time Value
XYZ 350	72¢	22¢	6¢	6¢
XYZ 400	38¢	38¢	22¢	22¢
XYZ 450	16¢	16¢	53¢	3¢

Comparing the time value component for the in-, at-, and out-of-the-money options, you can see that time value is relatively less for the put. For example, the in-the-money call has 22¢ of time value compared with 3¢ for the in-the-money put. So why the difference?

Remember how calls have an interest rate saving element? Well, the interest rate element for puts is negative. In other words, should you decide to sell your 1,000 ABC shares for $3.50 per share today, you would bank $3,500, which would start earning interest immediately. However, put takers only have the *right* to sell shares, and therefore don't receive any money through the sale of those shares until they exercise the right to sell. Thus, the put taker delays the earning of interest on that sale. On the other side of the transaction, the put writer delays the purchase of the shares, and therefore has the advantage of keeping his or her money in the bank. So put writers have no need to ask for a higher premium, as they are already earning the advantage.

Since put takers do not have the interest rate saving element, the time value of puts is relatively lower than for the same in-, at- or out-of-the-money call. Because of this, puts will be much quicker to lose time value as they move in- or out-of-the-money, as shown in Figure 7.4, opposite. As a taker, therefore, you need to be quicker to know when you have it wrong and need to exit. Also, since most takers exercise when there is little or no time value left on the option, as a put taker you will be more likely to exercise early—naturally, this means that the put writer has a greater chance of early exercise. Be warned!

So if the put taker has a negative interest rate element, how does this impact on the put premium over time?

As interest rates rise, the interest rate disadvantage becomes greater for the put taker. In other words, as interest rates rise, put premiums will fall (all things being equal).

Figure 7.4
Relative Time Value and Decay of Calls and Puts

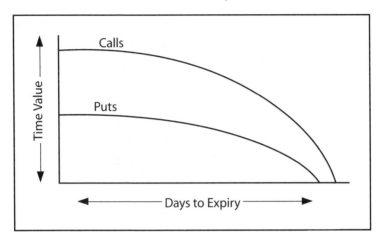

While puts will be relatively quicker to lose their time value than calls, the good news is that sharemarkets tend to fall twice as fast as they rise. I know that doesn't sound like good news for your shares, but it does mean that as a put taker you have a relatively good chance of making a quick profit if you get it right.

Other Pricing Factors—Volatility and Dividends

You might recall that calls trade in three main dimensions: price, time and volatility. So how does volatility affect put premiums?

Our definition of volatility says that it is a measure of how far a share price is likely to move around (either up or down) around an average share price over a specified period of time. The keys to this definition are the words 'either up or down'.

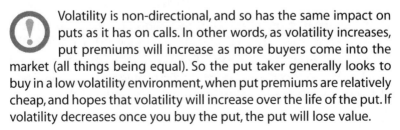 Volatility is non-directional, and so has the same impact on puts as it has on calls. In other words, as volatility increases, put premiums will increase as more buyers come into the market (all things being equal). So the put taker generally looks to buy in a low volatility environment, when put premiums are relatively cheap, and hopes that volatility will increase over the life of the put. If volatility decreases once you buy the put, the put will lose value.

The importance of volatility in both put and call buying is evident in the fact that the professional market usually doesn't refer to 'buying' calls or puts, but rather to 'buying' volatility. When you hear people say they are 'long vol' in a portfolio, this is what it means—that overall they have an expectation of volatility rising, and they will make a profit if this happens.

As far as dividends go, it's fairly straightforward. As the stock goes ex-div, the share price will fall. As put premiums have an inverse relationship with the share price, this means that the put premiums will rise (all things being equal).

If there is a dividend due on the shares underlying your particular put option, the price of the put will be relatively higher than if there were no dividend due. But beware. You will not see the put gain value because the shares have gone ex-dividend the day before. The expectation of the dividend is factored into the put premium from day one of its trading.

Table 7.1, below, summarises how the different pricing factors affect calls and puts. It is important to distinguish which have an inverse effect, and which have the same effect.

Table 7.1
Impact of Various Factors on Call and Put Values

Increase In	Effect	
	Call	Put
Stock Price	Up	Down
Exercise Price	Down	Up
Time to Expiry	Up	Up
Volatility	Up	Up
Dividends	Down	Up
Interest Rates	Up	Down

So you can see that puts gain value in a falling market, and therefore give you an opportunity to trade a bearish view. What are the best uses for puts within a share portfolio? We're going to find out in the next chapter how you can use puts for protection, for speculation and for reducing share exposure within a share portfolio.

8 THE BOUGHT PUT

PROTECTING YOUR SHARES FROM SHAREMARKET DECLINES

Chapter objectives:

- Reiterate the three ways of exiting a trade
- Summarise three reasons why you would buy a put
- Discuss option selection based on price and time
- Define delta and its use as a measure of risk/return
- Construct the bought put payoff diagram
- Provide practical ways of interpreting and applying the payoff diagram
- Differentiate between buying for speculation and for protection.

So far you know:

- The put taker has the right to sell 1,000 shares for a set price over a set period of time.
- Puts increase in value as the underlying share price declines (all things being equal).
- Puts decrease in value as the option gets closer to expiry (all things being equal).
- Puts increase in value as volatility increases (all things being equal).
- At expiry, a put is only worth its intrinsic value.
- You can take a put without having underlying ownership of the shares at the time you buy the put.

Obviously, you buy a put when you think the share price is going to fall. In other words, you are bearish on the underlying share price, and because of the effect of time decay, probably 'aggressively' bearish.

It is important to note that as the put taker, you do not have to have underlying ownership of the shares at the time you take the put. This is because all you have is a right to sell shares—no obligation at this stage. However, once you take up your right through exercise, you must have the underlying shares to sell. (Otherwise you will be tangled up in short-selling, and will have to abide by the Exchange rules in this regard.)

So how do you make a profit once you have bought your put?

Two Ways to Exit and Make a Profit

Just as it is with the call taker, the put taker can make a profit in two ways: either through exercising the right and selling the underlying shares through exercise, or by selling the put back onto the market for a higher premium. I emphasise the words 'by selling the put'— remember, because you have bought the put in the first place, you must sell it to liquidate your position.

> It is important to remember this. If you sell a call to liquidate your bought put position, all you will be doing is holding a bought put and a sold call in your portfolio. Not exactly the smartest way to try to exit your position! Remember those apples and oranges—puts and calls are completely different instruments. If you buy a put, you have to sell the same put to get rid of it.

Three Ways to Exit

Let's reiterate the three ways to exit your position, and the points to remember for each:

1. Exercising to sell the underlying shares

- You can exercise on any day, up to and including the expiry day.
- You will only want to exercise if your put option is in-the-money.

2. Selling the put and liquidating the position

- If you just want to make a profit out of the share price movement and have no intention of selling the shares, you are generally better off selling the put. By selling the put back onto the market, you keep the intrinsic value and also any time value remaining on the put. (But remember, time value will be relatively small for the in-the-money put anyway.)

■ Remember to tell your broker that the sold position is to liquidate your existing bought position.

■ The profit or loss is the difference between the initial premium you paid for buying the put and the premium received through the sale of the put.

3. Allowing the put to expire worthless

■ If at expiry there is no intrinsic value, the put will expire worthless.

■ If the put is in-the-money at expiry, and you have not sold the position or exercised it, you potentially can lose any premium that is left on it.

Be aware that the Exchange offers an automatic exercise facility to brokers. This means that if an option, either a call or a put, is a particular amount in-the-money at expiry, and has not yet been closed, the option will be automatically exercised. Now this may be good or bad, depending on whether you want to exercise or not—that is, whether you have the money to buy the shares if your call is exercised, or whether you own the shares already if your put is exercised. But at least it means you won't lose any remaining value on your option if you have failed to exercise or close out the position prior to expiry.

Please beware of two things with regard to automatic exercise. Firstly, it is important to note that the parameters for automatic exercise change regularly (for example, how far the option needs to be in-the-money for it to be automatically exercised), so it is important to either visit the Exchange website to see what the parameters are, or alternatively, ask your broker. Secondly, not all brokers offer the facility, so you also need to ask about it before opening an account with a particular broker. And whatever you do, don't rely on automatic exercise to exit your option. It's always best to monitor your position and make an informed decision about the way you want to exit it.

As I have mentioned before, it's usually a silly thing to let your option expire worthless. Generally it means you don't have any money or risk management rules in place, which is a guaranteed way of losing a lot of money over time. However, there is one occasion when you will celebrate when your put expires worthless—and that's when you buy a put for protection. Let's look at how that works.

Three Reasons for Buying a Put Option

So you have decided to buy a put option. There are three main reasons you might want to do this:

1. You want to lock in a price to sell shares at a future date

As previously mentioned, there may be times when you are worried about a potential share price decline. Rather than selling your shares immediately, you can lock in a selling price by buying a put option. By choosing the exercise price, you also select the selling price of the shares that you're happy with. You then have time to decide if you want to sell the shares, depending on what the underlying share price does over the life of the put. Remember, since you've paid the premium upfront, this cost must be subtracted from your final selling price.

So what happens if the share price falls over the life of the put? If the share price falls, the put option increases in value. You then have the choice of either exercising your put to sell the shares at a higher price than the current market price, or keeping the shares (which have declined in value) and selling the put back onto the market to recover a profit. This profit on the put offsets the loss taken on the shares. In this way, a put option acts like an insurance policy, allowing you to hold shares in a declining market and at the same time providing protection for your shares against the adverse price movements.

What about if the share price stays steady or rises over the life of the put? Clearly, the put will decline in value. Why does this make you happy? Because your shares are holding or increasing their value. If you bought that put as protection against a potential large decline, you will happily lose that premium in exchange for the protection it has given you over its life. It's the same for any insurance we take out—every year, we happily pay a premium for life insurance, house insurance and car insurance, and we are really glad when the policy expires without us having to call on it.

This strategy of taking protection for an existing shareholding is referred to as **hedging** by the professional market. A word of warning: while the theory of hedging is easy to understand, the actual process can be complicated, so it is vital that you get qualified advice before you undertake it (more on this later).

2. You want to speculate on an expected price movement in the underlying shares

You may not have underlying ownership of the shares, you might just want to make a profit out of an anticipated share price decline. By buying the put and selling it for a higher premium, you are able to take advantage of your market view without ever entering the sharemarket.

3. You want to reduce exposure to the underlying shares

If you are holding shares that are underperforming relative to other shares, but you aren't keen to sell them (they may, for example, deliver a good yield or may be pre-capital gains shares), you can effectively reduce exposure by buying a put option. In a similar way to the situation in the first point, above, if the shares continue falling in value your put increases in value and offsets the loss on the shares. This allows you to continue holding the shares in a falling market while at the same time making a profit that allows you to reinvest in another better-performing stock.

Right, by now you know:

- why you want to buy the put—that is, you're bearish on the underlying stock
- your reason for buying it—that is, for protection of an existing shareholding, or for speculating on the share price movement
- whether or not you will exercise the put or sell it back onto the market.

What are some of the other considerations before you buy the put?

Selecting the Put Option

Before you buy the put, you also have to know whether you're going to buy an in-, at- or out-of-the-money option, and whether it's going to be relatively short- or long-dated. The good news is the same rules apply for puts as for calls:

- At-the-money puts give you the highest return coupled with the best chance to get a return. In other words, at-the-money puts have the highest time value.
- At-the-money puts are generally the most actively traded and therefore give the benefit of higher liquidity.

- The more bearish you are, the more you would consider buying out-of-the-money puts.
- Which expiry month you select will depend on your view of the market, how much time you can afford to buy and how liquid the different expiry months are.
- Generally the most liquid months are the spot months and the three-month options.
- Be careful buying too much time. Options should be used for short-term exposure.
- Be careful buying put options in the last four to six weeks when time decay will be rapidly increasing.

You might recall that delta is another consideration when selecting which option to buy. While there are some similarities between the delta for puts and calls, there are also some differences. Let's go on and examine why they differ.

A Measure of Risk/Reward—Delta

You might recall from Chapter 4 that an option's delta is a measure of how much the premium will change in value when the share price moves. As a rough guide, a call option's delta will approximately be the following:

In-the-money	0.7 or 0.8
At-the-money	0.5
Out-of-the-money	0.1 or 0.2

The same absolute numbers hold for puts. The only difference is that delta for puts is negative, reflecting the inverse relationship between share price movement and put premium movement.

So, as a rough guide, a put option's delta will be approximately:

In-the-money	−0.7 or −0.8
At-the-money	−0.5
Out-of-the-money	−0.1 or −0.2

Figure 8.1, opposite, shows the relationship of delta to the exercise price of the option, and also how the relationship changes as the put

moves from out-of-the-money to at-the-money, and then to in-the-money.

Figure 8.1
Put Options Delta

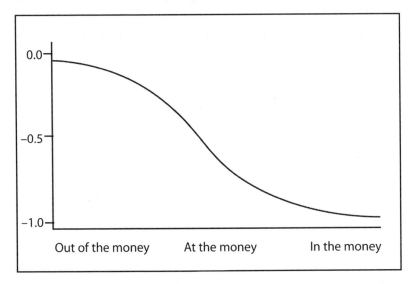

Further:

- Delta for puts ranges between 0 and –1.
- As a put goes deeper into the money, its delta approaches –1. At this point, the option will generally lose any remaining time value that is left.
- Be very careful buying out-of-the-money puts. Because of the relatively small delta, they will be very slow to respond to favourable share price movements.

The Option Payoff—Profit and Loss Profile for the Bought Put

By now you should be pretty familiar with option profiles, and the fact that they only take into account the intrinsic value of the option at expiry. Puts are where this gets tricky. Remember, a put has intrinsic value when you can sell your shares at a higher price than the current market—that is, when its exercise price is higher than the current share price.

In order to look at the put profile, let's assume that you buy an ABC MAR 400 put for 22¢. You do the calculations shown overleaf.

Share Price at Expiry	Intrinsic Value	Premium	Profit/Loss
$4.50	Nil	$0.22	$0.22 loss
$4.00	Nil	$0.22	$0.22 loss
$3.78	$0.22	$0.22	Nil
$3.50	$0.50	$0.22	$0.28 profit
$3.00	$1.00	$0.22	$0.78 profit
$2.50	$1.50	$0.22	$1.28 profit

Plotting the various profits and losses and then joining the dots results in the following profile:

Figure 8.2
The Bought Put—Buy ABC MAR 400 Put for $0.22

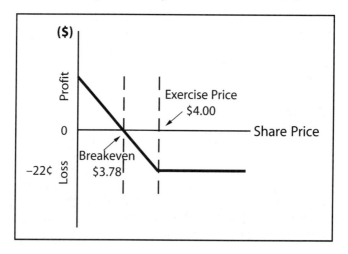

The profile for the bought put shows three really important things:

1. As the taker of a put, you can never lose more than the premium you pay

You can see that no matter how high the share price rises, you can never lose more than the premium of 22¢. The share price could rise to $1,000, and you would still lose only your initial premium. This is the major advantage of buying an option—you have limited risk.

2. The breakeven is at the exercise price minus the premium

As the share price starts to fall below your exercise price, your put starts to gain intrinsic value. However, you must recoup your initial premium before you can start making a profit.

3. The further the share price falls, the higher the profit you make

You can see from the profile that as the share price falls below your breakeven, you stand to make a larger and larger profit. Unlike the bought call, however, the bought put does not have unlimited profit potential, purely because the share price cannot fall further than zero. You can see the exact maximum potential profit on this trade. Should the share price actually fall to zero the breakeven of $3.78 is the maximum profit—that is, the $4.00 of intrinsic value less the initial premium cost of 22¢.

The Rules of Trading

While the profit potential for the bought put is not unlimited, it still poses the same problems in terms of the lure of potentially huge profits. Where do you take that profit? Luckily, the rules for trading puts successfully are the same rules for trading calls and you can review them by either re-reading Chapter 4, or at least reviewing the rules summarised at the end of this chapter.

In the meantime, let's take a more detailed look at the concept of hedging and how you can use it to protect your shareholding.

Hedging Your Bets

You read earlier that you can buy puts in order to protect an existing shareholding from potential share price declines. I mentioned that since the exercise price becomes the selling price of the shares, it makes sense that you select an exercise price that you're happy with. Further, the actual selling price of the shares is the exercise price less the premium paid (that is, the breakeven), since the premium becomes a transaction cost along with commissions and any other fees.

So, the breakeven tells you the final selling price of your shares, but it also tells you one more thing: how bearish you have to be before you decide to hedge your position. In other words, because of the high cost of hedging, unless you think the share price is going to fall further than your breakeven you don't hedge. There's no point, firstly because of the cost, and secondly because whenever you hedge you forgo the benefits of any positive price movement in the underlying shares.

Why? Because when you hedge, you take an equal but opposite position to your physical shareholding, and therefore keep your position delta neutral. Let's see how that works.

Delta Hedging and Rolling

By definition, hedging is an attempt to remove either:

- the specific risk (that is, company risk) of adverse price movements of a specific share within a share portfolio; or
- the overall risk of adverse price movements in the overall sharemarket from within a share portfolio.

Okay, so let's say you want to protect an existing share position from any adverse price movements below a certain share price (that is, your breakeven). The only way you can do that is to reduce your share's ability to change value; in other words, you keep the share price locked at a certain level. And the only way you can do that is to make sure the share's delta is neutral, or equal to zero—that is, that there is no movement in your portfolio's value when the share price moves. So how do you do that?

> The delta for a share is always 1. That is, when the share price moves, you would expect your shares to move one for one with the underlying share price movement. If you don't want your shares to move in value—that is, you want to fully hedge your position—you need to have one or more instruments in your portfolio with a collective delta of –1. This would mean that your net delta for that particular share within your portfolio would be zero (1 + –1 = 0). And if delta is zero, it means that there will be no price movement in that particular share across your portfolio, no matter what the share price does.

So how do you obtain a delta of –1? Well, remember those puts? Bought puts have negative deltas. This is why when you take a put against shares that you already own, it is referred to as hedging. But beware! If you buy an at-the-money put, it has a delta of around –0.5. So, if you want to fully hedge your position, you would need to buy two at-the-money puts—that is, in order for your puts to have a collective delta of –1, you would need 2 × –0.5. If you want to hedge with out-of-the-money puts, you would have to make sure that the collective delta equalled –1. If the collective delta is anything less than –1, –0.7 for example, you won't be fully hedged.

Now this might be a valid part of your strategy—maybe you don't *want* to fully hedge your position. But just make sure it is part of your strategy, and not simply bad management.

One of the most vital things to remember about delta hedging is that as the share price changes, the delta of those puts changes with it.

So, as the share price falls, the delta of the puts will get closer to –1. This is extremely important. If your two original at-the-money puts are now in-the-money, you must check your collective delta. If it is now –1.4, for example, you are over-hedged. In other words, your share position is now, in aggregate, bearish—your shares will gain value if the share price continues to fall and will lose value if it rises. Which is not the position you wanted to be in. You must do something to bring your collective delta back to –1. For example, you might decide to exit your two puts and buy one deep in-the-money put which reinstates your –1 delta. Alternatively, you might decide you no longer need to be hedged. The most important thing to remember is, you must adjust your collective delta for whatever your current strategy is—whether it is to remain fully hedged, partially hedged or to remove the hedge altogether.

This is the reason why delta hedging is also referred to as **delta rolling**. As the collective delta of your hedging instrument changes, you must roll, or adjust, your position to maintain your strategy. The most vital thing is to make sure that you are aware when you are over- or under-hedged. Otherwise, you will end up speculating on a share price move instead of removing the uncertainty.

Maintaining the correct hedge through delta rolling can become quite expensive. Transaction costs such as commissions become a deterrent for most people. And with the intricacies of changing deltas and the need for constantly monitoring and changing positions, it is essential that you get qualified advice before undertaking any hedging.

 When you delta hedge and your position's delta is zero, you are perfectly hedged against any adverse price movements. But remember, you are also perfectly hedged against any profitable price movements. This is why hedging is usually only undertaken when there is an anticipated large adverse price movement. In other cases the cost is usually much too high.

The reality is that not much hedging is undertaken in the Australian market. Most people, including the professional market, take puts purely for speculation. And not many do that either! Generally, puts tend to be more thinly traded than calls, probably because most of us are optimists and would rather wait for a rising market than sell into a falling one. But keep in mind that markets fall twice as fast as they rise, so there are many opportunities for profiting from those negative views.

Summary for the Bought Put Option

Action:	Purchase put, pay premium in full
Risk/Reward:	Limited risk/large reward that increases as the share price falls
Breakeven:	Exercise price minus the premium received
View of Market:	Bearish
Used for:	■ locking in a price to sell shares in the future (protection/hedging)
	■ speculating on an expected share price movement
	■ reducing short-term exposure to share price movements.

Key Rules for Trading Bought Put Options

1. Write down your reasons for buying the put option.
2. Define the large reward potential before you buy the put.
3. Define profit and loss targets before you buy the put.
4. Redefine the risk/reward ratio at the close of each trading day.
5. Do not build in profits as a buffer against loss.
6. Do not check the value of the put the day after you've sold it.
7. If you cannot decide whether to exit or not, ask yourself, would I buy this option today at its current premium and with its current risk/reward?

9
THE
SOLD
PUT

BUYING SHARES AT A LOWER-THAN-MARKET PRICE

Chapter objectives:

- Define the obligations of the put seller
- Differentiate between the objectives of the buyer and those of the seller
- Differentiate between the effects of pricing factors on the buyer and the seller
- Discuss option selection based on price and time
- Construct the sold put payoff diagram
- Provide practical ways of interpreting and applying the payoff diagram
- Discuss basic entry and exit rules
- Differentiate between selling for income and selling for entering the sharemarket.

Before we look solely at the put writer, let's reiterate the definition of the equity put option:

 A put option gives the taker the right, but not the obligation, to sell a standard quantity of shares at the exercise price, on or before the expiry date.

If the taker exercises the right to sell, the writer is required to buy a standard quantity of shares at the exercise price.

Using the example of a BHP JAN 900 put, this tells you that:

- the taker has the right to sell 1,000 BHP shares at the exercise price of $9.00 on any day, up to and including the expiry date in January

- the writer has the obligation to buy 1,000 BHP shares at $9.00 if the taker exercises the right.

So, for every put buyer (or 'taker') there must be a put seller (or 'writer'). And knowing that options are a zero-sum game, obviously the put taker and writer must have opposite views about where the share price is going over the life of the option. What is good or favourable for the put taker is bad or unfavourable for the put writer, and the risk/reward profile of the writer is a mirror image of that of the put taker. What does this mean for the put writer?

Buying Low and Selling High

Just like the call writer, the put writer is looking to earn income from selling the put to the taker. And like the call writer, the put writer hopes to be able to sell a high premium and then buy the option back for a lower premium later on. The first principle of making money in the market by buying low and selling high is maintained. Put writers are just doing it in reverse—selling high and then buying low later on.

So what happens to put premiums to make them fall in value?

Revisiting the Premium and the Major Pricing Factors

Remember, an option's premium comprises intrinsic value and time value. In order for the premium to fall in value, either intrinsic value or time value or both must be declining. So, let's reiterate the major pricing factors and how they affect the premium:

Increase In	Movement in Put Premium
Stock Price	Decrease
Exercise Price	Increase
Time to Expiry	Increase
Volatility	Increase
Dividends	Increase
Interest Rates	Decrease

What does this mean to the put writer? Well:

- if put premiums rise when the share price falls, the writer must make a profit when the share price rises or stays flat

- if put premiums fall due to time decay, the writer must benefit from time decay
- if put premiums rise when volatility rises, the writer must benefit from falling volatility
- if put premiums fall when interest rates rise, the writer must benefit from rising interest rates.

Remember that the effect of dividends is factored into the put premium at the start of trading, so this means if there is a dividend due on a particular stock, you will receive a higher premium for selling it in the first place. The effect of interest rates is minor in the low interest rate environment at the time of writing, and interest rates are usually slow to change, so their impact is often small even if they do change during the life of the put option.

Summarising the Zero-Sum Game

Looking at each side of the contract, and comparing the rights and obligations of the buyer and seller, we can summarise as follows:

Put Buyer	Put Seller
Otherwise known as a taker	Otherwise known as writer or grantor
Right to exercise and sell shares	Obligation to buy shares if exercised against
Pays premium	Receives premium
View is for market to fall	View is for market to rise or stay flat
View is for volatility to stay the same or rise	View is for volatility to stay the same or fall
Time decay hurts	Time decay benefits

Three Ways to Exit

When you sell a put option, there are three things that can happen:

1. *You can be exercised against and therefore have to buy the underlying shares*

As the put writer you ordinarily simply want to earn income from writing the put, so it's fair to say that you generally want to avoid exercise. Apart from the fact that it means you're going to take a loss on the trade (since you'll be buying shares in a falling market), there is also the cost of commissions and other transaction fees due on the share transaction (not to mention the cost of the 1,000 shares that you will be buying).

However, there may be times that you sell a put with the hope of getting exercised against when the share price falls. In this way, you buy shares at a set price that you're happy with (that is, the exercise price) and you receive some income as a reduction against the buying price. (More on this strategy later on.)

Whether or not you want to avoid exercise or ensure being exercised against, it is essential to know when it is more likely that you'll be exercised against.

As a writer, you can get exercised at any time. However, you are more likely to get exercised when there is little or no time value left on the option. In other words, you are more likely to get exercised close to expiry or when the put is deep in-the-money. This doesn't mean you can't get exercised earlier or when the put is out-of-the-money—it's just less likely. As a rule of thumb, you should start to get nervous when the share price falls below your exercise price. (More on this later.) In addition, virtually all put options that are at-the-money will get exercised close to expiry.

You might recall from an earlier chapter that put options have relatively less time value than call options. This means that puts will lose time value relatively quickly as they go into the money—good news if you want to be exercised against, not so good if you don't. And also remember that due to the process of novation (discussed in Chapter 2), there is no direct link between any buyer and seller. Sellers are randomly selected to buy the shares, and so it can be relatively difficult to ensure exercise if that's what you want. (Some tips on how to assess your personal chance of exercise can be found in Chapter 13, 'Using Financial Information to Optimise Trading'.) In addition, since each option is registered separately by the Exchange, if the put buyer has exercised 50 puts, anywhere from 1 to 50 separate put sellers may be selected. So if you were the seller of a 50 lot, you might find yourself exercised against anywhere from 1 to 50 options. It just depends on the luck of the draw.

2. You can close out your position by buying the option back before expiry (or before you are exercised against)

If the share price is rising or staying flat, and your put premium is worth less than when you sold it, you can close out your position by placing an order to buy it back. Your profit will be the difference between the selling price and the buying price of the put (less any cost of trading). Again, remember that when you place your order to buy with your broker, it is important to tell him or her that it is an order to close out, or liquidate, your sold position. You want the two orders to cancel each other out, not to end up holding one sold and one bought put.

Obviously if the shares are falling and your put has increased in value, you can still buy back the option and close out your position, but it will be at a loss. This might be appropriate to limit losses in your trading. (More about this later.)

Bear in mind that you can only liquidate your sold position if you haven't been exercised against. In other words, once you have been exercised against, there's nothing you can do but buy the shares from the put taker.

3. The put can expire worthless

In contrast to the put buyer, who loses all his or her premium if the put expires worthless, for the put seller this is the optimum result. It means that you have maximised your profit, and do not need to pay another commission to your broker for closing out the position. The option simply 'disappears', and you keep all the premium.

However, you are almost always better off closing the position before expiry. In terms of risk, there only needs to be a small change in share price or volatility to turn a worthless option into one with intrinsic value at expiry. Remember the client who lost a fortune on that 50 lot of calls, waiting for a few extra cents of premium? The same thing can happen with puts, especially considering the speed with which share prices can fall. And this speed is made even worse when there is a thin market to boot, as there is with puts.

The Earning of Income

Okay, so by now you know that as the put writer:

- You earn the premium for undertaking the obligation to buy shares from the taker if he/she exercises that right.

- You aim to sell a high premium first, then to buy the put back at a lower price.
- You make a profit if the share price stays steady or rises over the life of your option.
- You like it if volatility is relatively high when you sell the put, because it means your premium will also be relatively high. And you like it even better if volatility falls once you have sold the put, because the premium will fall with it, making it cheaper to buy it back later on.

Clearly, the put writer has the specific view that the share price will stay flat or will rise over the life of the put option. Rather than sit on the sidelines during this flat period, the put writer takes advantage of it by earning income through the receipt of the premium. In other words, as the writer, you speculate on your market view, probably never intending to transact through the physical sharemarket, but simply intending to make a profit on trading the option itself.

So if you earn the premium as your reward, what is the risk on the other side of your sold put?

The Option Payoff—Profit and Loss Profile for the Sold Put

By now you will be pretty familiar with an option profile, and the fact that it only takes into account the intrinsic value of the option at expiry. And since you already know that options are a zero-sum game and the risk/reward profile of the sold put is a mirror image of the bought put, you probably could guess that its profile is the reverse of the profile for the put buyer. That is, where the bought put makes a profit, you would see a loss for the put writer, and where the put buyer makes a loss, you would see a profit for the put writer.

Okay, so in order to look at the put profile, let's assume that you sell an ABC MAR 400 put for 22¢. You do the calculations shown opposite.

Plotting the various profits and losses and then joining the dots results in the profile shown in Figure 9.1, also opposite.

And again, the profile for the sold put shows you three really important things:

1. As the writer of a put, you can never make more than the premium you receive for writing the put

You can see from the profile that the put writer makes a profit when the share price rises. Unfortunately, the profit is capped, or limited, to the amount of premium received. It makes sense according to the zero-sum game—if the buyer has a limited loss potential, then the writer must have a limited profit potential.

Share Price at Expiry	Intrinsic Value	Premium	Profit/Loss
$5.00	Nil	$0.22	$0.22 profit
$4.50	Nil	$0.22	$0.22 profit
$4.00	Nil	$0.22	$0.22 profit
$3.78	$0.22	$0.22	Nil
$3.50	$0.50	$0.22	$0.28 loss
$3.00	$1.00	$0.22	$0.78 loss
$2.50	$1.50	$0.22	$1.28 loss

Figure 9.1
The Sold Put—Sell an ABC MAR 400 Put for 22¢

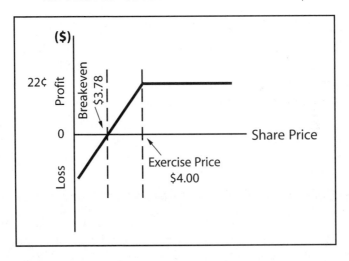

2. *The breakeven is at the exercise price minus the premium received*

In other words, as the share price starts to fall and the premium starts to increase, the premium received acts as a buffer against the loss for the writer. And in terms of the zero-sum game, buyer and seller have the same breakeven.

3. *As the share price starts to fall below the breakeven, you have the potential to make very large losses*

You can see from the profile that the put writer starts to make a loss as the share price falls. Unlike the call writer, the put writer doesn't face unlimited loss. The loss is, in fact, limited by the fact that the share price cannot fall further than zero; nevertheless, the loss potential is large, and increases as the share price continues to fall. The exact loss potential is actually the same as the breakeven—in other words, if the share price should fall to zero, this particular trade would lose $3.78 per share.

Is there anything about the profile for the written put that looks familiar? The profile, in fact, is the same shape and has the same profit and loss characteristics as the buy write discussed in Chapter 6. That's why we call the buy write a 'synthetic position'. A synthetic position is a strategy involving two or more instruments which have the same risk/reward profile as another strategy. In other words, you acquire the same exposure for the same risk. So the buy write is a synthetic written put.

The Rules of Trading—Profit and Loss Targets and Avoiding Exercise

Like the written call option, the profit potential for the written put is limited to the premium received. Unlike the written call option, the loss potential for the written put is not unlimited. However, the same problems of setting profit and loss targets exist for each. When do you take a profit? How far do you let a loss accrue? In addition, how do you avoid exercise?

Luckily, the rules for trading puts successfully are the same rules for trading calls. You can review them either by re-reading Chapter 5, or by at least reviewing the rules summarised at the end of this chapter.

Which Option to Sell—the Direct Risk/Reward Relationship

Before you sell a put, you have to know whether you're going to sell an in-, at- or out-of-the-money option, and whether it's going to be relatively short- or long-dated. Again, the good news is that similar rules apply for puts as for calls:

- You maximise your gain when selling at-the-money puts when you are neutral in your outlook.
- If you are slightly bearish, you might write an out-of-the-money put in order to avoid exercise.
- If you are slightly bullish, you might write an in-the-money put in order to capitalise on a large premium. Remember, this also holds

a high chance of immediate exercise (which might be good for the strategy discussed in the next section).

- Above all, there is a direct relationship between the amount of premium received and the amount of risk assumed—the higher the premium you receive, the higher your chance of exercise.

- The expiry month you select will depend on your view of the market, how long you expect the market to remain flat or to rise, and how liquid the different expiry months are.

- Since time decay benefits the writer, generally the best time to write an option is when time decay is at its worst—that is, in the last four to six weeks of the option's life.

So far we have been focusing on writing puts purely for the premium income. In this situation, avoiding exercise is high on your list of priorities. However, there might be a time when you *want* to be exercised against. And if you are, it can be an innovative way of buying shares at a lower price than the rest of the market. Let's see how.

Buying Shares Lower than the Rest of the Market

There may be times when you want to buy shares but think they are over-priced. You expect that there will be a small decline in the price once the market realises they are over-priced. Your plan is to wait for that short-term correction and buy the shares once they have dipped. Using a sold put, you could earn some extra income during this small decline and buy the shares at an even cheaper price.

Let's look at an example. Let's say you've been looking at ABC shares and they are trading at $6.50. You think they are over-priced and you don't want to pay $6.50 for them, but instead wait until they fall back to around $6.00. You expect them to decline within the next four to six weeks, so instead of just waiting for the fall, you decide to write an ABC JUN 650 put for 50¢.

Now, let's say you are right, and the shares fall to $6.20. You are exercised against and must buy the shares for $6.50. But originally I said that you didn't want to pay $6.50 for them! What have I done? Hopefully, you can see that because you earned 50¢ of premium for writing the put, your actual buying price of the shares is only $6.00, which is 20¢ lower than the current share price.

 This is why writing a put is referred to as an innovative way of buying shares for a lower price than the rest of the market. If it is set up correctly, you can reduce the buying price of your shares.

Of course, this isn't the only thing that could happen to you once you have written the put. What could go wrong?

- Firstly, the share price could keep plummeting once you have bought the shares. Okay, so this is always a risk when you buy shares, but remember, by having an expectation of exercise, you must be expecting the share price to decline. Is it smart to buy shares in a falling market? Only if the share price recovers.

- Secondly, you may not get exercised against even if the share price falls. Remember, there is random selection for exercise. You may be unlucky and not be exercised against quickly. In this case, you will be forced to close out the position at a loss, or to hold the sold put until expiry when you will be exercised against if it is deep enough in-the-money. And remember, if this is the case, it means you will be buying your shares at a much higher price than the current market price.

- Lastly, the share price might remain steady or even rise. This means that not only will you not be exercised against, you also won't be buying the shares. On the plus side, it also means that you'll be keeping the premium. And since your plan was to only buy the shares on a decline anyway, your disappointment at not owning the shares will be at least partially offset by the fact that you have earned some income over the period. Also, theoretically, you could keep writing puts as the market climbs, thereby earning more premium income to offset the lack of ownership of the underlying shares. I do stress the word 'theoretically'—remember, as the share price rises over a period of time, more than likely the demand for puts will decrease, thereby reducing the premiums and possibly the viability of writing the puts. You would only do this if it were worthwhile to you.

The majority of put writers tend to be happy to buy the shares if they are exercised against. Thus, while the risks involved in earning income this way are still large, put writers tend to feel more secure than call writers—that is, they feel better about buying shares and owning something which might increase in value if held long enough, rather than losing shares through exercise.

Whether you want to be exercised against or not, as the put writer you are neutral to slightly bullish in your market view. Either way, you can make a profit by selling the put. And for those of you who are aggressively neutral? Go on to the next chapter, and discover how you can combine the writing of puts and calls to earn even more income.

Summary for the Sold Put Option

Action: Sell put, receive premium in full

Risk/Reward: Limited reward/large risk that increases as the share price falls

Breakeven: Exercise price minus the premium received

View of Market: Neutral to slightly bullish

Used for:
- earning income in quiet markets
- speculating on an expected share price movement
- innovative way of buying shares at a lower-than-market price.

Key Rules for Trading Sold Put Options

1. Write down your reasons for selling the put option.
2. Decide whether you want to be exercised against, or whether you want to avoid exercise.
2. Define the large loss potential before you sell the put.
3. Define profit and loss targets before you sell the put.
4. Redefine the risk/reward ratio at the close of each trading day.
5. Do not check the value of the put the day after you have liquidated it.
6. If you cannot decide whether to exit or not, ask yourself, would I sell this option today at its current premium and with its current risk/reward?

---

10 THE SOLD STRANGLE

EARNING EVEN MORE INCOME IN QUIET MARKETS

Chapter objectives:

- Define the sold strangle
- Provide a practical example of combining options with share purchase
- Construct the payoff diagram
- Provide practical ways of interpreting and applying the payoff diagram
- Differentiate between selling for speculation and for share purchase
- Discuss basic entry and exit rules
- Explain the risks of a strongly rising or falling market.

By now you know that you can earn income in quiet markets by selling call or put options. Which option you choose to sell will depend on your view of the market—if you are neutral to slightly bearish, you would write a call option, and if you are neutral to slightly bullish, you would write a put option.

But what if you are aggressively neutral? It might sound odd, but for the investor who is completely neutral—that is, expects the share price to trade within a fairly narrow range—the sold strangle provides an opportunity to earn even more income.

Defining the Sold Strangle

The sold strangle is the simultaneous sale of an out-of-the-money call and an out-of-the-money put, both with the same expiry date (and naturally, both with the same underlying stock).

So why would you sell both at the same time? To answer that, you only have to look at each side separately. The optimum situation for the call writer is for the market to stay flat until expiry or at least go no higher than the exercise price. In this way, time decay eats into the premium, and the writer can close out the position later by buying it back at a cheaper price. Similarly, the put writer also wants time decay to eat into the premium so that it can be bought back more cheaply. And for the put, this is likely to happen when the share price stays flat until expiry, or at least falls no further than the exercise price.

Putting these two positions together, it means your view would be:

- for the share price to go no higher than the exercise price of the call option
- for the share price to go no lower than the exercise price of the put option
- for time decay to benefit the strategy
- for volatility to remain the same or, even better, to fall.

It's always easiest to look at an example. Let's say it's mid-May, and with ABC currently trading at $4.00, you sell the following strangle:

```
1  ×  ABC JUN 450 CALL   @   19¢
1  ×  ABC JUN 350 PUT    @    7¢
```

Because you have sold both options, you receive the premium for both. Your total income is 26¢.

To really understand this position, let's jump straight into the profit and loss profile.

The Option Payoff—Profit and Loss Profile for the Sold Strangle

Remember, in order to plot the position, you just need to calculate the profit or loss separately for the put and call at each share price, and then net it across the total strategy. So the calculations would be as shown in the table overleaf.

So plotting these various points would show the profile in Figure 10.1, overleaf.

Share Price at Expiry	Profit/Loss for the Call	Profit/Loss for the Put	Profit/Loss for the Strangle
$3.00	Nil	$0.50 profit	$0.50 profit
$5.00	$0.31 loss	$0.07 profit	$0.24 loss
$4.76	$0.07 loss	$0.07 profit	Nil
$4.50	$0.19 profit	$0.07 profit	$0.26 profit
$4.00	$0.19 profit	$0.07 profit	$0.26 profit
$3.50	$0.19 profit	$0.07 profit	$0.26 profit
$3.24	$0.19 profit	$0.19 loss	Nil
$3.00	$0.19 profit	$0.43 loss	$0.24 loss
$2.50	$0.19 profit	$0.93 profit	$0.74 loss

Figure 10.1
The Sold Strangle—Sell 1 × ABC JUN 450 Call at 19¢,
Sell 1 × ABC JUN 350 Put at 7¢

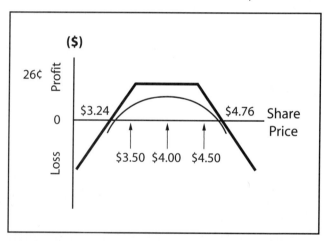

As with any options profile, it shows us three really important things:

1. The maximum profit potential is 26¢, the amount for which the strangle was sold

So just as it is for the call or put writer, the writer of the strangle will never earn more than the amount it is sold for on the day. But rather than earning only one income, the combined selling produces a total income greater than selling either the call or put alone.

2. Unlike the written call or the written put, the written strangle has two breakevens

And in fact, the two breakevens are the same breakevens as for the single written positions. In other words, on the upside, the breakeven is at the call exercise price plus the total premium received for the strangle. On the downside, the breakeven is at the put exercise price minus the total premium received for the strangle.

One of the most important things to stress about calculating the breakevens is that it is the total premium that is used to calculate them. In other words, as the share price starts to rise above the call exercise price, the position starts losing money. However, because of the earning of the combined premium, there is a buffer of 26¢ before you start taking a loss. On the downside, if the share price should fall below the put exercise price, there is still a buffer of 26¢ before the loss is realised.

3. Unlike the single written call or put, the written strangle has two potential maximum loss areas

And they are, in fact, the same as the individually written positions combined. In other words, on the upside, as the share price rises above the breakeven there is potential unlimited loss, and on the downside, as the share price falls below the breakeven there is a potentially large (not unlimited) loss.

So, the two greatest dangers for the written strangle are an unexpected large upward swing or an unexpected large downward swing.

The Hidden Risk of Exercise

Apart from the potential hip-pocket loss, there is another, hidden risk not shown by the profile—the risk of exercise. And that can be for either the call or the put, or, if you are really unlucky, both.

If you are exercised against on the call option, remember your obligation will be to deliver the shares at the exercise price, $4.50 (just as if you had sold the call singly). The total amount you receive will be the exercise price plus the two premiums ($4.76), and this is what makes the sold strangle so attractive. Rather than earning only one premium, you increase your return by receiving the two premiums, and they give you a bigger buffer against a rise in the share price. Even better if you already owned the shares—it becomes like a buy write, but at a sale price enhanced by two premiums, rather than only one.

On the downside, if you are exercised against on the put, your obligation will be to buy 1,000 ABC shares. But again, had you only

117

written the put, your buying price would have been $3.43. By writing the strangle, your buying price is reduced by the two premiums to $3.24. It's a really great way to buy shares at a lower price than the rest of the market.

So, like the individual positions, the sold strangle has the same rules:

- Don't write a strangle unless you are prepared to buy the stock.
- Don't write a strangle unless you are prepared to lose the stock.

Now a word of warning. If volatility increases while you are in the market, beware. The worst-case scenario for the writer of the strangle is a huge swing up, being exercised against on the call, then a huge swing down and being exercised against on the put. Can it happen? Rumour has it that that is how the sold strangle got its name. Huge unexpected price swings in the late 1970s saw many traders lose vast amounts of money from sold strangles. Exercise on one half and then the other saw many of them wiped out, or 'strangled' by volatility.

Exercise, as you know, is always a risk when writing options. However, there are ways you can protect yourself against adverse price movements and the risk of exercise—Chapter 14, 'Managing Your Position and Your Money', explains these in detail.

The Trading Range

So far we've looked at what happens if the share price rises above the call exercise price or if it falls below the put exercise price. But remember, there is a third thing the share price can do. And that's stay the same. If the share price stays exactly the same at expiry, you will simply keep the two premiums—it's the optimum situation for earning premium income.

There is one more great thing about the sold strangle. Because you have written out-of-the-money options, with exercise prices equidistant from the current share price, the share price can move around quite a lot and you will still keep your total premium.

In other words, looking at the profile on page 116, at what share price do you maximise your profit? Hopefully you can see that anywhere between the share prices of $3.50 and $4.50 (that is, the two exercise prices) you keep your total premium of 26¢. Just think about that. It is a huge range for a $4.00 stock. To put it in other terms, volatility can be around 12.5 per cent (that is, the stock can have a 50¢ movement either up or down) and you can still make your maximum profit. Not only that, but the share price can swing even further (between $3.24 and $4.76) before you start making a loss.

The Rules of Trading

Like the call writer and put writer, the main enemy of the strangle writer is greed—in this case, expecting to keep the total premium of 26¢.

Even though the sold strangle can be profitable across a wide range of share prices, the same rules apply for managing your written position:

- While the sold strangle is constructed with out-of-the-money calls and puts, usually the exercise prices chosen are equidistant from the current share price.
- Be careful writing too much time. While the extra premium is attractive, the risk of volatility changing over a greater period of time is also much greater. Always err on the side of caution when writing options with unlimited loss potential.
- Remember to revalue your risk/reward position at close of business each trading day. It's a really good way of judging whether you should exit a position or not.
- Decide whether or not you want to avoid exercise. Clearly, if one of your exercise prices is being breached, you need to think about exiting if you want to avoid exercise.
- The quicker you take your profit, the higher your annualised return is going to be. Don't stay in trying to get the last few cents of a trade. It's almost always better to take your profit, and see where there are opportunities to make a higher return in another trade.
- Since written strangles involve writing out-of-the-money options, always select stocks that have reasonable liquidity. This might be an obvious thing to say (as it applies to all strategy selection), however, since puts are relatively less liquid than calls, it becomes an even more critical part of your strategy selection when you write strangles. And remember, as a general rule, out-of-the-money options will tend to be less liquid anyway.

The written strangle has a lot of 'protection' against share price swings due to the use of out-of-the-money options. The large profitable trading range together with the receipt of two premiums makes it a popular strategy amongst option writers. Even more than that, it is an innovative way of adding stock to a portfolio at a cheap price, or of making quick high returns on stock purchase. Let's see how that works.

Combining the Sold Strangle with Stock Purchase

I first saw this strategy in the late 1990s when a broker friend ran a workshop with me. Since then, I have found it is one of the best strategies for share traders who want to combine options with their share trading.

Okay, the scenario is this. You've been watching ABC shares and they are currently trading at $4.00. You quite like the look of them and you wouldn't mind adding some to your portfolio—let's say 10,000 shares. However, you think that volatility is going to flatten out, and the shares will probably trade within a fairly narrow range for a while, if not even fall a little. Your analysis of past price action and volatility shows a probable range of around $3.50 to $4.50 over the next six weeks. You don't mind holding the shares if you can make some extra income over the period, or, on the other hand, losing the shares at a high return should there be some unexpected bullishness. You consider a buy write, but decide with the $1.00 potential trading range, you have the opportunity of increasing your returns by selling some puts as well. And if the price falls below the $3.50 range and you are exercised against, you won't mind adding more ABC shares to your portfolio.

Since you think the shares might range for a while, rather than buy the whole 10,000 shares at once you decide to only buy 5,000. At the same time, you sell five of the following strangles:

So your profile will look the same as the one earlier.

```
5 × ABC JUN 450 CALL @  19¢
5 × ABC JUN 350 PUT  @   7¢
```

And what does it show?

- Firstly, if the share price stays where it is at $4.00, you keep the whole five premiums of 26¢ (that is, $1,300). You're still holding onto the 5,000 shares, which have not shown any increase; however, by writing the strangles you have increased your return over the period. Should you be more optimistic at this stage, you might decide to use the $1,300 profit to offset the cost of purchasing the extra 5,000 shares. If you do, the average cost of your 10,000 shares becomes $3.87, rather than the original $4.00 you might have paid for them.

- Secondly, should the share price rise to $4.50 by expiry, your 5,000 shares have increased in value, and you also have the added 26¢ of premium which increases your return. The only disappointment might be the opportunity cost in not buying the extra 5,000 shares. However, the premium income received at least partially offsets the cost of buying the extra shares, should you wish to do so at this point. If you do, the average cost of your 10,000 shares becomes $4.12, which still provides an unrealised profit of 38¢ per share. On the other hand, you might decide to wait to see whether the shares will break the $4.50 range before buying more, or alternatively, sell more strangles to get more income.

- Thirdly, should the share price continue to rise above $4.50 and you are exercised against, your obligation will be to sell your 5,000 shares at $4.50. However, with the added premium, your total selling price is $4.76, and remember, you were originally quite happy to sell your shares if you could get a quick high return. And that return? Nineteen per cent before it's annualised. So if that was earned over a six-week period, it becomes around 165 per cent.

- Fourthly, if the share price falls to $3.50, you keep the whole five premiums of 26¢. Your 5,000 shares have lost 50¢ per share, so you are probably glad that you didn't buy the extra 5,000 shares. In addition, the 26¢ of premium earned helps offset this loss, making a total loss of only 24¢ per share.

- Lastly, should the shares continue to fall past $3.50 and you are exercised against, your obligation will be to buy 5,000 shares at $3.50. You're quite happy about this because it gives you your total of 10,000 shares, and even better, you get them at an average price of $3.62 as opposed to the original $4.00. So if the share price continues to decline, your unrealised loss will be greatly offset by the lower average buying price of the shares. It's even better if the share price recovers from here— you'll earn profits much more quickly due to the lower average buying price.

This strategy shows you the versatility of trading in options. It also demonstrates the advantages of using options to complement your share trading, rather than using them solely as an alternative to it.

Summary for the Written Strangle

Action: Sell out-of-the-money call together with out-of-the-money put, receive premiums in full

Risk/Reward: Limited reward/unlimited risk

Breakeven: Exercise price of call plus total premium received; Exercise price of put minus total premium received

View of Market: Aggressively neutral

Used for:
- earning income
- combining income with share purchase.

Pricing Factor	Effect on Written Strangle
Stock Price	Increase is negative for call, positive for put (reverse is true)
Time Decay	Positive
Volatility	Increase is negative, decrease is positive

11 Making Markets

Chapter objectives:

- Define the bid/ask spread
- Provide practical ways of using the bid/ask spread to interpret pricing and place orders
- Define the role and obligations of market makers
- Provide practical insight into the methodology of market makers
- Define the type of orders acceptable on the Exchange.

In order to trade effectively in any market, it is essential to 'buy low and sell high', as we've said before. Easy enough, isn't it? If you always buy low and always sell high, you will always make a profit. The hard part is deciding what is a 'low' price and what is a 'high' price. How do you know whether you're buying low and selling high? In other words, how do you know the real value of your option?

What is an Option Worth?

I heard a story once about a seeker of knowledge who set off in search of the answer to this very question. In his travels he hears of two wise men who are said by many to be very knowledgeable and experienced, and therefore will have an answer to this most perplexing question.

The first wise man, a famous guru, lives at the top of a mountain, high above the hustle and bustle of city life. After climbing and climbing for what seems hours, the seeker is able to find the guru and pose his question, "What is a call option worth?"

The guru answers immediately. 'It is not hard to prove that, using the Black-Scholes or Cox Ross Rubenstein Trinomial pricing models that the call option is worth...", and he quotes a rather complicated formula, adding, "Of course, this has to be modified somewhat in practice to take into account dividends, the value of early exercise and a few other technical details."

The seeker thanks the guru, not completely understanding the answer since it all seems a bit complicated and subjective, and decides to find the second guru. The second man lives in the middle of a city, surrounded by the hustle and bustle of noise and activity. Once the seeker is able to get his attention, he asks the question again, "What is a call option worth?"

The market maker turns around, and answers immediately, "That depends. Are you buying or selling?"

The Bid/Ask Dilemma

Okay, so this anecdote raises another problem with using pricing models to calculate what your option is worth. A pricing model gives you one theoretical fair value for your option, but if you look at a price screen or a newspaper quote, the first thing you notice is that there is not one quote but two: a 'bid' price and an 'ask' price. So what does this mean?

Basically, the bid price is the highest price that someone is willing to pay to buy the option. The ask price is the lowest price that someone is willing to receive for selling the option. If your pricing model has correctly estimated the fair value of the option, and the market reflects this fair value, you would expect the fair value of the option to be roughly in the middle of the bid/ask spread.

Clearly, if the ask price is higher than the bid price, no trade can take place. In order for you to buy the option immediately, you must be willing to pay the ask price. For example, let's say we look up a BHP JUN 1100 call, and discover a bid/ask of:

BID	ASK
36	40

This means that while someone is willing to buy the call for 36¢, someone else is only willing to sell it for 40¢. If you wanted to buy this option immediately, you would have to put in a bid to buy it for 40¢. In other words, you will always buy at the ask price, and sell at the bid price, if you want to trade immediately.

If you are willing to wait to buy your option, you can, of course, put in a lower bid than the current ask price and hope that market forces change enough for you to buy your option. However, if you want to have a good chance of getting your order filled, you might place your bid between the current bid/ask quote, say for 38¢, in this way hoping that a seller might come in who is willing to forego the extra 2¢, and meet your price.

One way of deciding on a fair price for the option is looking to see what the last trade is—that is, the last price for which the option was traded. Just be careful—this might have been hours ago, and prices may have moved substantially. However, if the last trade is within the current bid/ask spread, there's a good chance of getting your order filled at that price.

In this example, there is a price spread of 4¢—that is, the difference between the bid and the ask is 4¢. Were you to buy the option and immediately sell it, you would lose 4¢ on the trade. Maybe this doesn't sound too bad, but what if this spread was 20¢? Would you still buy the option?

The price spread between the bid and the ask is always a cost to you, and is an excellent indicator of liquidity, or activity, in that particular option series. Be careful as you see this spread widening. It means the cost of trading is getting more expensive, and more importantly, that liquidity is drying up.

The Exchange monitors the width of all bid/ask spreads so that they do not exceed certain limits. You can check the current width regulations via the Exchange website, or alternatively, ask your broker.

You'll find that if liquidity dries up sufficiently, there will be no quote for that particular series of option. If there is no current quote, you can ask your broker to put in a quote request to the market makers.

So who are these market makers, and what are their obligations?

The Market Makers

Market makers are professional traders who work for themselves, or for an organisation, and trade in options in order to make money.

They trade on their own accounts and for their own risk, and compete against each other in the market.

In addition, under the Exchange Business Rules, they are required to provide bid/ask quotes in particular options, either on a continuous basis or on request. In this way, liquidity is increased in the market—you might be trading with another private investor in the market, or you might be trading with a market maker taking the other side of your order.

Market Maker Obligations

Generally, market makers are assigned two or more stocks in which they must meet certain obligations. These obligations are to:

- make a market on a continuous basis only; or
- make a market in response to quote requests only, or
- make a market both on a continuous basis and in response to quote requests.

Be aware that while the market makers are there to add liquidity to the market, there are certain limitations to their obligations:

- Where the market makers have the obligation to make a continuous market, the obligation only extends to three calls and three puts in the closest two expiry months. In other words, they do not have to provide orders beyond these 12 series.
- In the stocks where the market makers have an obligation to make a continuous market, they only have to meet their obligation 60 per cent of the time. And this is reduced to 50 per cent if they are also providing quote requests for those stocks.
- In the stocks where the market makers have an obligation to make quote requests, they only have to meet their obligations 60 per cent of the time. This is reduced to 50 per cent if they are also providing continuous orders for those stocks.
- The orders they are placing only have to be for minimum quantity, and can be placed at the maximum spread width.

 There are some stocks which may not have market makers. When you start trading, it is essential to ask your broker which stocks do, because you have a much better chance of finding liquidity wherever you find the professional market.

Quote Requests

Let's say you have decided to buy a particular option in the market. You ask your broker to give you a quote, and he responds by saying there is no current quote on screen. You then ask your broker to put in a quote request, which he does electronically, and you wait on the other line for your broker to get back to you with the quote. Market makers who choose to make a market in response to quote requests must respond, at the time of writing, within 30 seconds, by giving a bid/ask quote for a minimum number of contracts. Your broker then comes back with the quote, and you have 30 seconds within which to respond by buying the option. Naturally, if you don't like the quote you don't have to accept it.

Now, a word of caution. If you are forced to ask for a quote request, what is the likelihood that the price you are getting is the option's fair value? In other words, ask yourself why there is no quote on the screen. The answer is that there is no liquidity in the option series. Why is there no liquidity in the option series? More than likely:

- the option is deep out-of-the-money
- the option expiry is too far in the future, e.g. nine months away
- there is little demand/liquidity for the underlying stock and therefore the options for that stock
- there are no market makers competing naturally in the options for that stock.

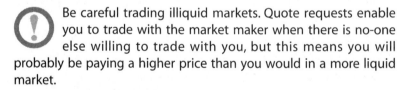 Be careful trading illiquid markets. Quote requests enable you to trade with the market maker when there is no-one else willing to trade with you, but this means you will probably be paying a higher price than you would in a more liquid market.

How the Market Makers Make Money

Okay, so the market makers are trying to make money by trading options, just like you. How do they do it?

Basically, by providing the bid/ask quotes, the market makers are trading the spread between the two prices. Let's use the previous example of the quote:

BID	ASK
36	40

If this quote is given by a market maker, essentially what it is saying is that he or she will buy from you for 36¢ and sell to you for 40¢, thereby making a profit of 4¢. Doesn't sound like much, but market makers do not have to pay commission to a broker, and in addition, they pay cheaper Exchange fees to trade. So if they can trade for large volumes, and with little risk, they can make lots of money.

From the market makers' viewpoint, if they can buy and sell options quickly they have little risk in the market. The risk to them is that they buy a call option for 36¢, the liquidity dries up, and they are forced to hold the position overnight. This means risk that the underlying stock might move unfavourably and they might lose money.

 If a market maker sees that liquidity is drying up, he/she will widen the bid/ask quote.

In the previous example, the spread might be moved to:

BID	ASK
32	44

This means they are willing to buy for 32¢ and sell for 44¢, thereby making 12¢ on the trade. The increased reward that they are demanding is a direct reflection of the increased risk they perceive from the lack of liquidity. And who is paying the cost of this risk? You, if you decide to trade with them at those prices, and the market remains thinly traded until you exit.

How Wide Can It Go?

As discussed earlier, the Exchange sets rules as to how wide the bid/ask spread can go. Clearly, this is to prevent market makers from making ridiculous quotes in thin markets.

The spread width is determined by:

- the liquidity in each underlying stock
- the premium range in each underlying stock.

 As a general rule, maximum spreads are between 5¢ and 20¢, with the higher premium range showing wider maximum spreads. Because liquidity and premium range in the underlying stock can change, it is important to speak to your broker about any changes. Alternatively, the Exchange publishes updates on its website.

In addition to the width of the spread, each stock also has a minimum number of contracts for which the market maker must give a quote. This means that when your broker asks for a quote request, the market maker will give a quote based on this minimum number. For example, if you ask for a quote request, and the current minimum number established by the Exchange is 10 contracts, the market maker will automatically give you a quote based on buying or selling 10 contracts. Let's say that quote is 8-14. This means he/she will either buy 10 contracts for 8¢ or sell 10 contracts for 14¢. If you want to get a quote request for more than this minimum amount, it is important that your broker informs the market maker—you just might get a better quote if the volume is higher. For example, if you want to buy 50 contracts, and your broker informs the market maker of this at the time the quote request is placed, you might find the market maker quoting 9-13. This means that he/she will either buy 50 contracts for 9¢ or sell 50 contracts for 13¢.

The minimum number of contracts is published by the Exchange and can change from time to time. Make sure your broker informs you of the minimum requirements before you ask for a quote request.

Pricing an Option

You've read so far that the market makers have the obligation to make the bid/ask quote when natural market forces (that is, the rest of the market participants) have failed to make it. You've also read that as liquidity dries up these quotes widen. But how do the market makers know where to place the spread in the first place? In other words, how do they price the option?

Market makers use pricing models such as the Black-Scholes or binomial models to determine the fair value of the option, and then place their quotes around that price. The Derivatives Trading Facility (DTF), which is a screen trading system similar to the Stock Exchange Automated Trading System (SEATS), has a function which allows market makers to automatically update their prices as the various factors, such as share price and volatility, change during the day.

Basically, prior to the start of trading each day, the market makers input their pricing parameters of share price, time to expiry, volatility, interest rates and dividends into the model, and it automatically prices all the option series in which they quote. These quotes then appear on the DTF screen at the start of the trading day, providing you with quotes as soon as the market is open. In addition, the market makers have the ability to change any parameters during the trading period; so, for example, if they see volatility increase, they can automatically update all their prices quickly and easily by one change on the computerised system.

These quotes automatically update throughout the day as the share price moves and as other market participants enter the market. However, bear in mind that if there are no other market participants, the quotes you see are market maker quotes. If there are several market makers making a quote in the same option, you might be tempted to believe that this is a true competitive market. Be aware that this is not necessarily the case. After all, if all market makers use a pricing model to calculate the fair value of the option, then most probably all market makers are coming up with the same fair value. The only reason there will be a difference in the option quote is if one market maker is willing to adopt more or less risk than the others.

Types of Acceptable Orders

Earlier, you read about the bid/ask spread and how to place an order to buy immediately or at a specific price. When you instruct your broker on the type of order you would like to place, it is important to know the specific language to use.

The two most common types of orders are market orders and limit orders.

 A **market order** is an order to buy (or sell) at the best possible price immediately. In other words, in the previous example of the bid/ask spread of 36/40, if you placed an order to 'buy at market', you would be buying the option at 40¢.

A **limit order** limits the price you pay for the option. It instructs the broker to buy (or sell) at a specified price or better. For example, if the bid ask spread is 36/40, you might place an order to buy at '38 limit'. This would instruct your broker that the maximum you want to pay is 38¢. (Clearly in this case, not enough to buy the option immediately.)

In addition, you can instruct your broker to place orders as follows:

- Good for day—the order remains until the end of the trading day if not filled immediately.
- Fill and kill—if part of the order is transacted immediately, the rest is cancelled.
- Fill or kill—the entire quantity must be traded immediately or the order is cancelled.

If you are placing a spread, such as the short strangle strategy discussed in the previous chapter, or a buy write, it is essential that your broker places the two sides of the order as one order, or 'combination'. This instructs the market to fill both sides of the order simultaneously or not at all, thereby ensuring that you aren't left with only one side filled, and a different strategy and risk profile than intended.

Your broker will quote a price based on the total premium cost or receipt for the overall position, rather than two separate prices for each 'leg' (that is, each side of the transaction).

Usually, one of the worst things you can do is to try to 'leg in' or 'leg out' of a strategy—that is, place each side of the strategy as a separate order, trying to get a better price than by placing it as a strategy. Apart from the dangers of getting hit on one side and not the other (that is, getting one side of the order filled and not the other), the professionals have already priced the strategy. They know what it's worth, and there's no way you're going to be able to get a better price for it. So it's always much better to be safe than sorry.

Of course, as soon as there's a rule, there are times when you should break it. There may be times when it is smart to leg in or out of a strategy. For example, if you have written a strangle and the share price rockets up, it might be appropriate to exit the call in order to avoid exercise. At the same time, you might want to hold onto the put (assuming it's not worthless or time to exit), or alternatively, you might want to roll one or both of the positions into another sold strangle. In addition, there may be times when, rather than doing a buy write, you buy stock first and then write the option once the stock has had a run up (and the calls have inflated in price). In this way, you might receive a much higher premium for the call, and also have less risk of exercise. Remember, the key to options is their flexibility.

12 MANAGING RISK

YOUR MARGIN FOR ERROR

Chapter objectives:

- Discuss the concept of margining in regard to risk management
- Define the two components of margining
- Provide a practical method of estimating risk margin requirements
- Differentiate the requirements of covered call writers and naked call and put writers
- Define forms of collateral acceptable to the Exchange
- Provide quick margining facts.

Writers of calls and puts both take on substantial risk, since each position can result in large losses if the share price moves against them. Naturally, the Exchange is quite nervous about these potential losses. After all, since it stands as middleman between the buyers and sellers, how can it offer a performance guarantee to both sides of the option contract unless it has some form of guarantee that losses will be paid?

Managing the Risk of Writing

In order to provide protection to option buyers and to prevent writers trying to 'ride out' increasing losses that they cannot afford to pay, the Exchange manages the risk of unlimited loss potential by a process referred to as margining.

In basic terms, margining is a process which calls upon writers to pay losses every day as they make them. This means that when the writer eventually decides to close the position, the Exchange is confident that the writer has the necessary funds to liquidate the position at current market prices.

The Exchange's margining system, TIMS (Theoretical Intermarket Margining System), calculates each individual client's margin requirements at the close of business each day and then reports these requirements to every broker before start of business the next day. The broker pays the total margin requirement through to the Options Clearing House (OCH) at the Exchange by 11.00 a.m. the next day and then must collect the margin monies from each client. Each client then has 24 hours within which to pay the margin to his or her broker.

The fulfilment of each contract is guaranteed by the fact that the Exchange already holds the margin money from the broker, and thus doesn't have to wait the additional 24 hours for the client to pay it directly. So you can see from this that, in fact, it is the broker who takes on the direct responsibility for collecting the margin money, and the direct risk should a client default on a margin payment.

The Margining Process

I'd like to use the call writer as the initial example of how margins are calculated, even though the concept is the same for call and put writers. Looking at the call writer, you already know that:

- the writer receives the premium for having the obligation to sell shares to the buyer on exercise
- the premium is credited to the writer's account at the start of the trade.

Theoretically, once you sell the call you immediately have an unlimited loss potential (assuming you don't already own the shares). What if the share price shoots up tomorrow and you suddenly are facing a $10.00 per share loss on the position? Even worse, what if you cannot afford to pay that loss?

In order to cover that loss, the Exchange calculates two parts to the margining process. For every written position:

The total margin requirement = Premium Margin + Risk Margin

Let's look separately at how each component operates.

Premium Margin

One of the risks in selling a call is the actual day-to-day movement in the premium amount. For example, say you sell a call today for 72¢ and tomorrow it's worth $1.28. You're taking a loss. At some point, you are going to have to close the position by buying back the sold call and realising that loss. What if you keep holding the written call, hoping for the share price to turn around, and it doesn't? The loss could be huge by the time you actually close the position (theoretically, unlimited).

 In order to manage the risk of the day-to-day movement in premium, the Exchange calls the premium margin. The premium margin for a written call is the market value of that option at the close of business each day.

For example, if the call is valued at 50¢ at the close of business, the premium margin payable the next day on that position would be 50¢. This means that as the writer, you would have received 50¢ for selling the call, and would therefore pay a 50¢ margin call—then, if you had to close the position the next day by buying back the call, you would have already paid 50¢, thereby leaving you with no further monetary obligation. You would be 'square' as far as your profit/loss situation went at the start of the trading the next day.

Now let's say that on day two the closing market value of the call is 75¢. The premium margin requirement would now be 75¢, or 25¢ more than you have already paid. You would be margin called for 25¢ and you would need to pay that amount within 24 hours to your broker. If on day three the closing market value of the call were 60¢, you would receive a credit of 15¢ back into your account on the morning of day four. If you then closed the position on day four by buying the call for 60¢, you would realise a 10¢ loss—you sold the call for 50¢ and you are buying back the call for 60¢. And guess what? You've already paid that 10¢ loss through the process of margining—that is, you've paid a total of 75¢ in margin calls (50¢ + 25¢) and you have received a total of 65¢ into your account (50¢ + 15¢).

You can see by the calculations opposite how this process keeps your account squared at current market values.

	Day 1	Day 2	Day 3	Day 4
Closing Market Value	50¢	75¢	60¢	60¢ (liquidation)
$ Amount Required to Close Out Position = Margin Required	50¢	75¢	60¢	—
Margin Calls	—	50¢	25¢	+15¢
Total Margins Paid = $ Amount to Close Out Position on Previous Day	—	50¢	75¢ (50 + 25)	60¢ (75 – 15)

So the process of premium margining is a way for the writer to lodge enough cover for daily adverse movements in the actual premium. But there's a second risk in the market. What if there is an unusually large daily movement in the premium, and the next day you are called for a huge premium margin which you cannot afford to pay? To cover this possibility, the Exchange calls the second component of the total margin requirement: risk margin.

Risk Margin

The risk margin is a measure of how far the share price can adversely move against your position in one day. It looks at the worst-case scenario for the call writer, using the historical volatility measure to determine the maximum probable daily price movement for the underlying security, and then theoretically revalues the option at that share price.

Once the theoretical value of the option is calculated, the risk margin is the difference between the option's current market value and this new theoretical value. In other words, you pay the additional amount as if the worst-case scenario has already been realised, and this is held as a security bond in the event it should happen. The risk margin is then added onto the premium margin for your total margin requirement.

Bear in mind that the risk margin, like the premium margin, can change daily. It really depends on what the underlying share price is doing while you are in the market. Generally, the risk margin is the

135

largest part of the margin requirement, since it is payable even when the market direction is benefiting the writer. Remember, it is the worst-case scenario performance bond.

> While the Exchange calculates risk margin requirements for you, it is essential for you to understand how they are calculated and to be able to estimate your requirements before selling the call. Risk margins become a cost to you when writing calls, since this is money that must be held by the Exchange while you are in the trade.

Remember the example of the client waiting for 2¢ further profit on his written calls? This is where the smart traders take their profits early, because there can be substantial amounts of money tied up in margin commitments. And if you have to have money tied up in margins, it is always smarter to have it tied up where you can make 50¢ premium income rather than a lousy 2¢. Not only that, but there is nothing more frustrating than having to close a position too early because you have not allowed for margin requirements within your money management strategy.

Now while I have said you need to understand margins, it can be very difficult for you or your broker to calculate exact total margin requirements, since the whole process involves very complex calculations and pricing models. You won't know the exact total margin amount due until the day after you sell the call, when OCH uses TIMS to calculate it for the broker.

So the question is, if you have to take margins into account within your money management strategy, and it becomes a vital part of the estimation of risk within a portfolio, how do you know if your risk-carrying ability and available risk capital will allow you to sell the call in the first place? The answer is, there is a way to effectively estimate risk margin requirements. Any broker should be able to do this for you, or alternatively, it is a good idea to learn how to do it yourself.

The Exchange publishes what's called a margin interval calculation for every stock, and this is basically the historical volatility measure for that stock. This is a critical indicator for the call writer, because it allows you to estimate your risk margin requirement.

The margin interval is a percentage which tells you how far the share price could move from its current price. Let's say XYZ shares are currently trading at $4.00 and the margin interval for XYZ is 10 per cent. This means that XYZ shares could move up or down by

40¢ (that is, 10 per cent of $4.00). As the call writer, you aren't concerned about a fall in the share price, but you would be worried about the share price rising 40¢ (the worst-case scenario) since it means your call would also go up in value. But how can you tell how much your call would go up in relation to the share price, without using a pricing model? Well remember delta? Delta gives you that approximate measure.

 By multiplying your option's delta by the amount the share price can move up via its margin interval, you can calculate an approximate risk margin requirement for your written position.

For example, if your option's delta is 0.5 and the stock can go up 40¢, it means your option could move up by around 20¢. So you would be likely to be called for a risk margin somewhere close to 20¢. Your total margin commitment, therefore, would be the current market price (premium margin) plus this 20¢. Remember, this is only an estimate. As delta increases, it means that your risk margin requirement is going to increase with it and the reverse is also true. But at least it gives you a ballpark figure to use within your money and risk management strategy.

 As the name suggests, the risk margin is a way of managing and monitoring the unexpected risk of holding a written option—that is, of managing and monitoring the large potential risk profile. Be careful as your risk margin requirements continue rising—it's a sure sign that your risk is rising, and also that you are probably staying in the market too long. The margin interval is a good indication of this. If the Exchange is increasing the margin interval, it means that volatility is rising—a sure-fire way to lose money as an option writer.

Since the risk margin basically tells you the maximum possible loss you might suffer on your position, it is therefore a critical indicator for helping you set your risk and money management strategy. Remember that undefined risk? The risk margin helps define it. After all, the Exchange calculates the risk margin as a way to manage its overall risk in the market, so why reinvent the wheel? You might as well use the same indicator the professionals use to manage and monitor risk.

While margins are a way to keep your losses up to date, be aware that they can mask the full extent of the loss before it is realised. It may not be too painful to meet those individual margin calls, or even the final loss to close the position. So it is essential for you to monitor the total loss as you go, especially in reference to your money and risk management strategy.

> Be careful if you find yourself getting repeated margin calls. Not only does it mean you are taking a collective large loss, it is usually a sign that you are staying in the market too long. In addition, repeated margin calls are often a sign that you do not have an exit strategy in place, or if you do, that you might need to re-evaluate whether it leaves you open to too much risk.

Covered Writing versus Naked Writing

You might recall that the covered call writer or buy writer does not have the same unlimited loss profile that the naked writer has, due to the underlying ownership of the shares. Because of this, covered call writers are not subject to the payment of margins as long as they lodge their shares through OCH via their brokers. The margins are still calculated by OCH; however, your broker will realise that you have sufficient cover for your position, and therefore will not need to physically call you for any margins.

> While you are not subject to margin calls as a covered call writer, beware of becoming lazy in terms of monitoring your position. It's a good idea to still ask your broker for your daily margin requirements, because this is a good way to monitor the risk of the position.

Unfortunately, put writers will always be naked. In other words, it doesn't matter how many BHP shares you own if you write a BHP put, since your obligation through exercise is to buy more. You must pay margins in order to cover your losses and potential losses. And how can you pay for these margins? Well, cash is always good, but the good news is you don't have to lodge cash. The Exchange accepts other forms of collateral, which may increase your returns if used instead of cash.

Collateral Damage

The Exchange accepts several forms of collateral, and since any collateral lodged is literally security for your broker's margin obligations to OCH, it is possible that your broker may accept other additional collateral.

The Exchange finds the following forms of collateral acceptable at time of writing:

1. Cash.
2. Shares and other ASX traded securities. For example, there are certain eligible instalment warrants which can be used as collateral. Bear in mind that any securities are subject to a 'haircut', or reduction in their face value, of approximately 30 per cent. This means that, for example, should you lodge a range of securities with a total face value of $10,000, OCH will reduce this by 30 per cent, leaving you with $7,000 to cover any written positions. This haircut provides further security for OCH and you against a sudden fall in the value of the collateral securities.
3. Bank guarantees from OCH-approved banks.
4. Austraclear pledged securities, which include bank negotiable certificates of deposit, bank bills of exchange, non-bank promissory notes or certificates of deposit and other money market securities which have been lodged with Austraclear and have been pledged to OCH.
5. Stock bought on margin through certain margin lenders.

If you are planning to use cash as your cover, it is often a good idea to open a cash management account with your broker. You then give your broker permission to withdraw funds from the account to pay margins on your account.

Having a cash management account helps you in two ways. Firstly, if you decide to go away on holidays and forget to provide margin cover in the event you need it, you might find your broker closing your position the first time you fail to meet your margin call. Not such a great outcome if your strategy was to stay in the market. A cash management account prevents this, since your broker has the authority to withdraw funds to pay your margins. But one word of warning. Margin payments are a good way of monitoring your positions. Having a cash management account which allows you to 'forget' your margins just might make you lazy about monitoring your positions.

Secondly, and possibly more importantly, a cash management account allows you an immediate record of your trading success. In other words, it allows you to keep track of your exact starting capital, and whether your trading is profitable overall or not. This is especially handy when it gets to taxation time and your accountant needs a direct record of your losses and profits for the financial year. Believe me, when you are trying to review trading statements and open position statements from your broker, it is really handy to have one account dedicated to the financial standing of your trading.

Additional Quick Margining Facts

- In addition to the margining requirements, the Exchange also calls a once-only minimum lump sum payment of around $2,000 from writers. This amount is not used for margin payments; rather, it is held by your broker while you are in the market and is returned when you exit. Again, it acts like a performance bond while you are in the market and adds another dimension of protection against losses.

- There are two things to stress in regard to this payment. Firstly, it is not set on a per contract basis, but as a once-off amount. So theoretically you could write one call and pay $2,000, or you could write a 50 lot and still pay $2,000. Secondly, it is a minimum amount. Together, these two things mean that more than likely your broker is going to call a higher amount than this, especially if you plan to write large volumes of options.

- The Exchange has the right to call intra-day margins in fast-moving markets. This means that if there are dramatic movements during the day, rather than wait to call margins the next morning your broker will call you for margin payments during the day. The timing of when you need to pay these may change according to the circumstances, but be aware that if your broker asks for payment by a certain time you must pay by that time, or your broker is allowed to close out the position.

- While TIMS calculates the margin requirement for each individual option position held in your account, it also recognises that, for instance, a stock cannot go up and down at the same time. This means that if you are holding written calls and puts across the same stock within a portfolio, TIMS calculates collateral offsets which reduce the total margin amount that you need to pay. In addition, offsets can occur across the same or different stocks, expiry dates, and so on, and can considerably reduce the cost of trading.

 Since offsets allow you to trade more effectively with the risk capital you have, it's usually more cost-effective to keep your trading in one account and with one broker. So, unless you are getting some other benefit by having several trading accounts across different brokers, think about using one broker and one account only.

While offsets provide clear advantages to your trading, be aware that they are another reason why it is difficult for you or your broker to calculate exact risk margin requirements. If you trade a large portfolio of options across a lot of different stocks, if you write as well as buy options or do more complex strategies, it will be very difficult to calculate requirements. It means that more than likely, you will overestimate your margin requirements unless your broker has access to more sophisticated portfolio tools for estimating risk.

Alternatively, you might find that your broker calls a higher amount from you than the OCH calculation. This is a legitimate practice where the particular broker uses a different risk management system and calculation to OCH. Different brokers may, therefore, call higher margin calls than others. You should ask the broker what his or her margin requirements are prior to opening an account, since increased margins increase the cost of your trading.

13 USING FINANCIAL INFORMATION

TO OPTIMISE TRADING

Chapter objectives:

- List the different types of information and tools available
- Define financial terms found in the press
- Provide practical ways for you to use financial information
- List available websites
- Tips to enhance your paper-trading.

Okay, so by now you're keen to start trading. You might even think it's a good idea to try some 'paper-trading' before you commit your money to the market. But how can you paper trade or commit money to actual trading without access to current market information? How do you get option prices, updates on market information, access to more educational material, or find tools like pricing models to aid your trading? And once you find the market information, how do you know what's useful to you and what's not?

Finding Price and Technical Information

There are many types of market information and tools available, and which you choose to use will depend on how active and close you want to be to market information, how much analysis you want to do yourself, how much time you have to

142

spend on trading, and how much money you have to spend to get your particular financial information and tools.

Traders often ask me what the best system or method is—unfortunately, this is as unique to the individual as everything else about your trading. However, the general rule of thumb is, the more active you are, the more analysis you want to do yourself, the more time you have to spend and the more money you have, the more sophisticated system you will need to buy. Just beware—being close to the market does not necessarily make you a better trader. In fact, it can have quite the opposite effect, since the closer you are, the more your emotions are likely to impact on your trading decisions.

For most traders, the only requirement is the ability to check on price information at least once, preferably twice, a day. That usually can be done via your friendly broker, or via websites that show limited price information. After all, you already have your exit rules in place—all you need to do is keep an eye on when they might get activated or when you might need to reassess your position.

Generally, you can obtain the following types of market information:

1. Live data

As the name suggests, this gives you a live feed into market prices, volatility, volume, etc., so that you can see all the information movement as it happens. This is the sort of information your broker uses.

Live data can be quite costly, since it requires specific computer equipment, packages, lines, and so on, and generally is only required by the professional full-time trader.

2. Delayed prices

This gives you access to market information on a delayed time basis, often around 20 minutes behind the actual market movement.

Delayed prices can be found for free on a large number of websites but are also available via pagers that can be hired or bought.

3. Close of day price information

Close of day information generally includes information such as the open, high, low and close, as well as volume and open interest. Close of day information is usually downloaded via a modem and used to update technical analysis packages. It can also be found on various websites, as well as in the print media.

Trading Tools

Once you find the price information you require, you also need some way of analysing and interpreting it. There are a variety of different trading tools which will help you do this.

Technical analysis software

These are software packages which provide charts and other technical indicators for use in analysing market activity and to help you with selecting your entry and exit points.

There are many different packages available and many different analytical tools. It is important to view as many as possible before buying, since they can vary widely in ability, computer requirements and cost.

Some websites also contain technical tools. Depending on the website, these are often free to access.

Other useful tools

Pricing models, strategy profilers, position management and margin estimators can also be useful trading tools. These can generally be found for free on most market websites.

> More than likely, all you will need during the day is access to delayed prices and the good news is, you can get these free from various websites, including the Exchange's. If used in conjunction with close of day price information, found either via websites or the financial press, you should be able to adequately track your positions. In addition, once you become more active, a technical analysis package can give you a good way of selecting your trades and money and risk management strategy. (More on this in Chapter 14, 'Managing Your Position and Your Money'.)

For more information on how you can obtain demonstrations of the various tools available, speak with your broker or the Exchange. The Australian Technical Analysts Association (www.ataa.com.au) can also be a useful place to start.

Easy Access—the Financial Press

One of the easiest ways to access market information is via the newspapers. They're cheap, are produced every day and you can get them delivered straight to your door. And most of the information you need is listed in them—you can get pricing, measures of volume, measures of delta and measures of implied volatility. The main downside in using them is that you will be using retrospective information—that is, the information they contain is based on the previous day's trading. No good to you if you plan to enter the market tomorrow but only have yesterday's price information, and the market has moved overnight. In addition, the information is somewhat limited—unless the option has traded on that day the newspaper won't print any price information. However, if you can accept these limitations, newspapers provide a valuable source of daily information, particularly to the paper-trader. Used in conjunction with live pricing quotes available via your broker, they give you a good starting point for designing your trades and entry and exit points.

 The two newspapers that provide market information are *The Australian* and *The Australian Financial Review*.

They both provide similar information:

- all call option information listed separately to put option information—that is, the complete listing of call options will appear before the full listing of the put options for a particular stock
- option information listed alphabetically according to the underlying stocks—that is, ABC stock will be listed before CDE stock, etc.
- last sale price of the stock
- listed option expiry months up to nine months in advance— that is, if it is August and an option trades in quarterly expiry cycles, the newspaper will show SEP, DEC and JUN expiries (as long as they are currently listed and trading)
- fair value of the option
- last sale price of the option
- volume traded for that day
- open interest in each series
- implied volatility for buyer and seller
- delta
- annualised percentage return.

So what do all these terms mean, and how can you use this information in your trading?

Understanding and Using Market Information

Let's assume the following information is in the newspaper:

```
ABC PTY LTD LAST SALE PRICE $10.30
```

Expiry	Strike Price	Fair Value	Last Sale	Vol 000s	Open Int	Implied Vol Buyer	Implied Vol Seller	Delta	Annual % Return
JUL	9.97	0.44	0.43	242	1916	25.95	24.35	0.72	23.69
JUL	10.21	0.29	0.29	90	1462	26.29	25.08	0.57	39.77
JUL	10.44	0.17	0.16	168	1553	24.99	24.08	0.42	29.62
JUL	10.68	0.09	0.08	54	949	24.32	23.64	0.27	15.74
JUL	10.92	0.05	0.04	37	554	24.21	23.63	0.16	7.79
JUL	11.16	0.03	0.02	35	1431	25.78	25.29	0.10	4.57
AUG	10.21	0.47	0.45	35	902	26.43	25.66	0.58	28.36
AUG	10.44	0.35	0.34	34	484	25.58	24.95	0.49	23.92
AUG	10.68	0.25	0.23	69	516	24.90	24.44	0.39	16.75
AUG	10.92	0.17	0.16	8	347	24.77	24.33	0.30	11.62
SEP	10.44	0.48	0.46	64	3456	25.50	24.97	0.52	20.55
SEP	10.92	0.28	0.27	426	3636	24.78	24.39	0.37	11.99
SEP	11.16	0.23	0.20	11	1056	25.55	25.20	0.30	9.63
SEP	11.39	0.17	0.14	20	2833	25.43	25.12	0.25	7.28
DEC	9.49	1.28	0.81	100	791	22.32	21.53	0.80	10.21
MAR	9.73	1.26	0.92	450	17	19.28	18.75	0.78	9.69

1. Expiry

The first thing you notice from these expiry dates is that ABC trades in a quarterly cycle (that is, MAR, JUN, SEP, DEC), but that it also has a spot month option. And it must currently be July—hence the addition of a July and August spot month option. This tells you that once SEP starts trading, there will be an OCT option listed. But in the meantime, you can only trade the expiries listed above.

2. Strike Price

The strike or exercise price is generally listed in even numbers. So you can see by these strikes that there must have been a bonus or rights issue, or some other form of capital reconstruction, which has changed the strike prices to odd amounts—JUL 997, for example. And what else does this immediately tell you? That the number of underlying securities might have changed as well. Before trading any of these options, you must ask your broker how the change in strike price might have affected the number of underlying securities. Otherwise you might find yourself doing a buy write only to discover that you don't have the right number of underlying securities to be fully covered.

 When selecting which strike price to trade, remember that the paper only shows options that have traded on that day.

For example, you can see that the JUL and AUG 1068 options are listed, but there's no SEP 1068 option showing. This doesn't mean that it's not listed by the Exchange—only that it didn't trade on that particular day. Make sure you speak with your broker to get a full list of available strikes for all expiries before selecting your trade.

3. Fair Value

Since the fair value is the option's theoretical price using a pricing model, this gives you a guide as to where you might want to trade. Used in conjunction with the bid/ask, you can see whether the market is over- or under-pricing the options. Generally, the fair value will be within the bid/ask spread—if it's not, it might be an indication of poor pricing in the market, or that the market has moved overnight.

Just be careful if you are calculating your own fair value and comparing it to the newspaper's. Different pricing models will give a different fair value calculation. You need to know the model used before you can compare it to yours.

4. Last sale price

As the name suggests, this is the last price at which a sale was transacted. It gives you a good idea of the price at which you might be able to get an order filled. Just be careful—there's no way of knowing at what time of the day the option was traded.

 Generally, if prices or volatility haven't moved since the last sale, the last sale price should be somewhere at or between the current bid/ask quoted by your broker. If it is outside the bid/ask, it means prices have moved since this was recorded.

You can see that generally the last sale is close to the fair value for most strikes. This will be more likely wherever there is sufficient liquidity in the market. But be careful. See the DEC and MAR series? There is a huge difference between the last sale price and the fair value, and this means that the market has moved since those options were traded.

5. Volume 000s

Volume shows the number of option contracts that have traded during the day. Just be aware that while the newspapers show volume in 'thousands', this is the number of underlying shares, not the number of options that have traded in the day. So, looking at JUL 1068, volume shows as 54—this means that 54 option contracts were traded for that series, not 54,000.

Volume is a good indicator of liquidity. The higher the volume traded, the higher the liquidity, and the more likely that option prices will be more efficient. So you are more likely to get filled at a better price. For example, if you compare AUG 1068 to AUG 1092, you can see that the 1068s have much more liquidity than the 1092s.

As you can see from the table, generally volume is greatest around-the-money. This will almost invariably be the case, across all option series and classes—another great reason to consider around-the-money options first.

6. Open Interest

Open interest is the number of buyers and sellers who are still in the market and haven't closed out their contracts. For example, looking at SEP 1092, open interest is 3636—this means that there are 3,636 buyers and 3,636 sellers who are still holding open contracts and are yet to close their positions. If you buy an option today, and no-one else opens or closes a position, open interest will increase by one. And if you close your position tomorrow and no-one else opens or closes another position, it means open interest will decrease by one tomorrow.

Open interest is another good indicator of liquidity, since it means that apart from a new trader coming into the market, you also have the ability to trade with someone who might decide to close their current contract. Looking at the SEP 1092 again, it shows you that there are 3,636 potential traders who might take the other side of your transaction, not to mention any new traders who might want to enter the market.

For the writer, open interest gives a good indication of your personal chance of exercise. The higher the open interest, the lower your chance of getting exercised against if a buyer exercises.

That is, if you write a SEP 1092 option, you have a one in 3,636 chance of getting exercised against. Contrast this against the SEP 1116, where you have a one in 1,056 chance of getting exercised against, and you might decide to choose the SEP 1092 instead if you want to avoid exercise. Of course, if you want to be exercised against—for example, if you are writing puts in order to buy shares—the reverse is true. That is, you might select a lower open interest series in order to give yourself a better chance of being exercised against.

7. Implied Volatility Buyer/Seller

Implied volatility uses the market price to calculate the market's perception of the current level of volatility. There's a separate quote for buyer and seller, because the calculation uses the bid and the ask. Some traders average this out to get an estimate of current volatility; however, if there is sufficient liquidity in the market, you'll find that generally the quotes are reasonably close together anyway.

Remember, volatility is expressed in percentage terms. For example, looking at JUL 997, it shows that volatility is somewhere around 25.95 per cent and 24.35 per cent.

 Implied volatility on its own doesn't tell you much. But if you can compare it against historical volatility measures, it gives you an indication of whether volatility is likely to rise or fall from where it is.

So, looking at JUL 1116 with an implied volatility of around 25.78 per cent and 25.29 per cent, if you compared this to an historical volatility of 75 per cent it suggests that volatility is more likely to rise from here. This might be a good time to buy options, since if volatility rises once you have bought, the option premium will rise with it. Alternatively, if historical volatility were 12 per cent, it would suggest that volatility is more likely to fall from here. This might be a good time to sell options, since if volatility falls once you have written the option the premium will fall with it. At the least, you might decide not to be buying in such a high volatility environment, since premiums will be over-inflated already.

Remember, comparing implied and historical volatility isn't necessarily a sure thing—volatility doesn't have to fall just because it's relatively high. But it does give you an indication of what it's more likely to do.

Another useful way of using implied volatility is to track it over time—is it rising or falling? Is there much difference between the market's perception of closer-to-expiry options versus longer-term ones? For example, see how DEC and MAR options are showing relatively lower volatility? Remember, you want to buy options in a low volatility environment, and sell into a high one. If volatility is already relatively high for short-term versus long-term options, it might not be the right time to buy that option, since it means the premiums are already inflated.

8. Delta

Delta is a measure of how much your option is going to move when the share price moves. It is also a good indicator of chance of exercise for the writer.

> Remember, the higher the delta, the deeper the option is in-the-money and the more likely a buyer is going to exercise. So the closer the call's delta is to 1, and the closer the put's delta is to –1, the higher the chance that particular option will be exercised by a buyer.

9. Annual Per Cent Return

The annualised percentage return shows the return for the writer. It assumes that the stock stays exactly where it is by expiry, and shows the relative returns that are achievable.

It goes without saying that as the writer, if you are trying to decide between two different option series you might want to select the one that will give you the highest return. Just be careful—generally, the higher the return, the more risk you will be adopting with it. And also make sure that the return is worth it to you. See the JUL 1116? If you aren't making much better-than-bank returns, it might not be worth taking on all that risk.

> One further indicator that is no longer shown in the financial press (though still available through your broker) is the series high and low. Basically the high and low show the highest and lowest option premium that was traded for that particular series of option since day one of trading. The series low can be a great indicator for the writer, in showing the lowest breakeven for the series, and the first share price where a buyer is likely to exercise.

This is how it works. Let's say the following call options have been traded with the following series lows:

JUL 1000	@	25¢
JUL 1025	@	19¢
JUL 1050	@	8¢
AUG 1000	@	32¢

Calculating the individual breakevens using the series lows would show:

JUL 1000	Breakeven	@	$10.25
JUL 1025	Breakeven	@	$10.44
JUL 1050	Breakeven	@	$10.58
AUG 1000	Breakeven	@	$10.32

In other words, if you are the writer of the JUL 1000, you are unlikely to get exercised against before $10.25—the lowest breakeven of anyone who has been in the market. If you write the JUL 1050, you are unlikely to get exercised before $10.58, and so on. So ask your broker to tell you the series low for any option that you're writing—it just gives you that added level of comfort against exercise.

Website Material

The number of useful market websites and the amount of information available on them is huge. Market information on websites includes educational tools such as booklets and courses, trading tools such as pricing models, strategy profilers and margin estimators, trading games, price information, links to other sites and news updates. They are one of the quickest and most efficient ways of accessing day-to-day market information.

Although the number of possible websites is enormous, the following list is a good starting point. They focus generally on equity products, but you might find some of their links to futures websites also helpful:

- www.asx.com.au
- www.comsec.com.au
- www.cboe.com
- www.nyse.com
- www.hotcopper.com.au

Paper-Trading

Once you have gained access to market information, you might want to use it to help you get a feel for the market before committing any money to it. One of the easiest and most popular ways of getting to know the market, how pricing affects options, market depth and the mechanics of trading, is via paper-trading. Paper-trading is basically simulated trading which allows you to choose your trades, place your entry and exit rules, and have a trial run without the risk of real loss. So, it gives you the ability to learn from your mistakes, without learning from any monetary repercussions. And that's my biggest criticism of it.

Your biggest education from any practice environment is in the mirroring of the actual risk/reward that will face you in the real world. Let's face it, if you're approaching your trading without any real fear of loss, it's going to be relatively easy to make unemotional decisions that return you a profit. And yet you know that your emotions will have a huge impact on your trading results in the real world. It's a little like playing computer games—you're quite willing to go into that cave to face the three-headed giant, because you know you're not really going to get your head smashed in the process. You might not be as confident if there were real risk attached to it! In other words, the decisions and actions you take would be different in the real environment. And even though you may end up becoming a swordmaster and killing the giant in the game, it is unlikely that in real life you could do the same. In the same way, paper-trading does not necessarily make you a better trader—just a better paper-trader.

Having said that, it's not that paper-trading won't help you—you just need to be aware of its limitations. If you want to paper-trade, the following suggestions might be more beneficial to you:

1. Attach some real risk to your paper-trading. That is, have something real as the repercussion of making profits and losses. That could mean attaching a dollar-for-one-thousand-dollar value to the losses—for example, if you lose $1,000, put $1 into a jar, or give it to your spouse. Or it might be that if there is an overall loss, you have to take your partner to dinner, or vice versa if there is a profit. Maybe you pay 1 per cent to 100 per cent of your paper profits to your favourite charity. Just make sure that whatever the real risk is, it is sufficient for you to get a feel for the real emotions of making losses and profits in the market.

2. Don't do paper-trades that you couldn't afford to do in the real trading environment. This means you have to take into account your real risk-carrying ability and starting bank, and the margin requirements for the positions.

3. Beware the risk of exercise. Obviously it is pretty difficult to be exercised against when you paper trade. But you must still attempt to take exercise into account when you are paper-trading written positions. Make up some rule for it—for example, that you are exercised against when the breakeven for the series low is hit.

4. Calculate all transaction fees as if you are paying them. They include commissions, Exchange fees, exercise fees, etc.

5. Use the bid/ask spread instead of the fair value for entering and exiting trades. In other words, if you sell, use the bid price, and if you buy, use the ask price. It's amazing how a few cents here and there will have a huge impact on your trading results overall. And check to make sure that the option series traded that day—if the options didn't trade, you should assume that you could not have been filled on that day, regardless of the fair value quoted in the paper.

6. Remember to stick to all your money and risk management rules. That's the whole point of the exercise—to see whether they work for you over time.

7. Don't just evaluate overall profits and losses. Remember, the most important thing is to see what sort of a return you are getting. Does it match your trading objectives? Do you need to adopt more or less risk? Do you need to change your risk or money management rules, or your perceptual filter? Your overall objective is not to be right about the trades—it's to make a return that you'll be satisfied with.

8. Make a note of any psychological or emotional effects during your paper-trading. Did you brag about being right to one of your friends? Did you feel anxious, nervous or angry making a loss? Did you feel the need to follow the crowd? Did you ignore your perceptual filter? Keep a journal of any effects, as it will be an invaluable record of probable real-world effects once you start your real trading.

So now you have access to market information, and you're almost ready to start trading. But first, you need to have a good money and risk management plan in place. So, let's look at how you can design one that suits your trading style, objectives and pocket.

14

MANAGING YOUR POSITION AND YOUR MONEY

Chapter objectives:

- Introduce the concept of risk/reward
- Enable you to gauge your risk-carrying ability
- Outline generic risk and money management rules
- Discuss strategies to minimise loss
- Discuss strategies to maximise profits
- Define the four most dangerous trading habits
- Introduce the 10 rules of successful traders
- Introduce the concept of technical analysis as a perceptual filter
- A word on black box trading.

You know by now that options are an ideal way to change the risk profile within your portfolio. You've already read how put options can be used to reduce risk; how the buy write can give some limited downside protection; how you can get highly leveraged returns from buying calls and puts; and how the writing of calls gives you unlimited risk in the market. But what sort of trades should you be taking on within your portfolio? How much risk can you afford to adopt? What happens if you increase or decrease risk in your trading? How do you know if a certain level of risk will enhance your trading or put you at too much risk? And what happens to your potential rewards if you change your risk profile?

The Concept of Risk/Reward

Risk/reward is always a tricky thing. For example, you know that the writer of a call option has unlimited risk with a limited reward.

Doesn't sound too smart, does it? On the other hand, the buyer of the call has potentially unlimited reward with a limited risk. Sounds a whole lot smarter. But you know that the reward is not really unlimited, just undefined. So what is a good risk/reward?

Let's start by looking at the concept. Once you start trading, you'll find that brokers tend to talk about these two in relative terms. That is, you might hear things such as, "This strategy has a risk/reward of 1/3". So what does that mean? Is that a 'good' risk/reward? And what, in general terms, *is* a good risk/reward?

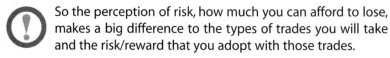 Using the above example of a risk/reward of 1/3, it simply means that you will be risking one unit to make a potential three units. If the value of that one unit is $1, it would mean you are risking $1 to make $3; if the value of that one unit is $10, it means you would be risking $10 to make $30; and if the value is $1,000, it means you are risking $1,000 to make $3,000.

So the question is, is the reward of potentially making $3,000 worth the risk of losing $1,000? The only person who can answer that is you. Risk/reward is a very personal thing.

Let's say that there's a trade in which you can risk a dollar to make a dollar. Would you take on the risk? Let's say you would. What if in the next trade you could risk $10 to make $10. Would you take on this risk? Assuming you would, what would you do when the next trade's risk is $1,000 to make $1,000? Sounding riskier to you? Well in fact, it's no riskier than risking one dollar to make one dollar— in other words, the risk/reward is still 1/1 for each of these trades. The only difference is the amount of money you can potentially lose, and whether you can afford to lose it.

I have asked these questions of traders, and have found that different traders will stop at different amounts—I've even had one trader say he'd risk $1 million to make $1 million! But that's because he could afford to lose the $1 million. If you cannot afford to lose $1 million, the risk/reward of 1/1 is too much to adopt for that particular trade.

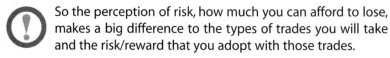 So the perception of risk, how much you can afford to lose, makes a big difference to the types of trades you will take and the risk/reward that you adopt with those trades.

Overall, whether a risk/reward is good or bad will depend entirely on you. However, in general terms, the potential return should be reasonable to you. And let's face it, unless you are making a lot better than bank returns, the risk you're adopting will make no sense—better to leave it in the bank! On the other hand, all trades should be able to pass the sleep test. Worry and anxiety are good indicators of inexperience and lack of knowledge on the trade, an adopted risk that is too high, or of having no plan in place. Or more than likely, it reflects a combination of all of three.

Risk-Carrying Ability

Before you can answer the question on which risk/reward you can afford to take on, you need to have an idea about your own personal risk-carrying ability.

 Your risk-carrying ability is basically a gauge that tells you how tolerant you are to recover from losses and therefore how risky your investments can be. This ability is inextricably linked to your own unique needs and goals for your trading.

Ask yourself these three questions:

1. What do you want to accomplish?

2. When do you want to achieve it?

3. What level of risk are you willing to adopt?

Your needs and goals might include such things as the need for:

- security
- flexibility (e.g. toward change through different life stages—having children, leaving work, etc.)
- liquidity
- income
- capital growth
- retirement income.

In addition, your personal risk-carrying ability is basically determined by the following criteria:

- your age
- your income
- your ability to continue earning that income
- the value of assets that you already own
- the risk profile of the assets you already own
- your financial responsibilities.

In other words, the younger you are, the more money you are earning, the higher your potential is to continue to earn a high income, the larger the value of your existing assets, the lower the risk profile of your existing assets and the fewer your financial responsibilities, the higher the risk you can adopt within your trading.

Of course, the irony is most traders in the options market come into the market with the reverse of the ideal risk-carrying ability profile, because of the attraction to the 'high reward' aspect of trading. You must never lose sight of the other side of the equation—that is, higher reward has to mean higher risk. And it is essential that you know how much you can adopt.

Your Personal Risk-Carrying Ability, Needs and Goals

It's a good idea to identify these things before you start trading, because not only do you need to identify the types of trades and risk/reward you can adopt, your broker needs to know these things as well.

In fact, it is a requirement through the Corporations Law that your broker not only make a list of your needs, goals and risk-carrying ability prior to making a trading recommendation to you, but that he/she also regularly update these as your circumstances change. This is what's known as the 'know your client' requirement, and it is the key to providing you ongoing sound financial advice.

Generally, your broker is likely to want to make a record of the following things:

1. Your investment history and objectives:
   - the types of investments you have previously undertaken
   - whether income, capital growth, or liquidity is your main concern
   - the general timeframe you usually consider for your investments;

2. Your risk-carrying ability;

3. Your personal circumstances and individual values:
   - planning for retirement
   - planning to take leave from work
   - planning for children's education
   - the need for ethical investments;

4. Your financial situation:
   - assets owned alone and jointly, e.g. family home, other property investments, shares, cash, other investments

- current and potential liabilities, e.g. mortgage, borrowings on other investments
- current income and expenditure of you and your spouse
- indication of future income and expenses
- capacity to save
- tax status
- asset and income protection held
- level and type of superannuation;

5. Your personal details:
- your age
- your current occupation
- family commitments
- social security eligibility;

6. The types of option trades you see yourself undertaking:
- buying options for speculation
- writing options for income
- buying options for protection
- buy writing for income.

It's a good idea to copy and complete this list so that you're ready with the information when your broker asks for it. After all, he or she cannot place a trade on your behalf until this information is provided. So it's much better to be prepared.

I have spoken with many clients who find their broker's 'know your client' questioning too intrusive. However, just remember that the more information you supply your broker, the more adequately he or she can advise you. And even if you don't plan on taking your broker's advice but intend to do your own analysis, it is still vital to objectify your trading objectives and risk-carrying ability in this way. After all, you might be surprised at how much risk you really can afford to adopt—or even more importantly, how much risk you cannot afford to adopt.

Risk and Money Management

Okay, so you've provided all the information, have profiled your financial situation, your needs and goals, and your risk-carrying ability. Now what?

Once you have decided on the types of options trades you are likely to undertake, you need a plan to help you meet your goals. And that plan needs to take into account risk and money management that can protect your capital against loss. After all, statistics say that out of 10 option trades, you will probably only make a profit out of three or four of them.

So what does that say about the size of your profits and the size of your losses? No wonder everyone says, "Cut your losses, and let your profits run." But how do you do that?

 Without a risk and money management plan, you run the risk of liquidating too early, not diversifying enough or overtrading, and trading all high-risk trades in order to get the high return, eventually destroying your starting capital with accumulated losses. A good risk and money management plan allows you to stay in the market, surviving those six or seven losses in a row if need be, in order to make the three or four profits that will give you your overall high return. Your plan should increase your risk when you are trading well and decrease it when you aren't.

In other words, a good risk and money management strategy is one which allows you to stay in the market long enough to maximise your profits, to exit trades early enough to minimise your losses, and which suits your temperament for trading. It needs to be consistent and you need to use it consistently, so that if used over a period of time it will return you overall profits.

The Components of a Risk and Money Management Strategy

A risk and money management strategy allows you to decide:

- how much starting capital you will allocate for trading
- how much money you will have at risk at any point in time
- how you will limit losses
- when you will take profits.

Allocating Starting Capital

The first thing to say is that according to reasonable investment principles, you should only trade with risk capital—that is, money you can afford to lose.

But how much to start with? There's no real answer to this, except to say that money makes money. The more money you have to invest, the more trading you can do, and the higher the likelihood of success. After all, if you only have $1,000 to start with, it is going to dramatically reduce your trading choices, and more than likely you'll be forced to risk a rather large amount of this at once in order to get any sort of leverage and chance of profit in the market. But only you can say how much of your total investment capital you're willing to start with for your trading. Once you have decided that, you then need to decide how much you will have at risk in the market at any point in time.

Money at Risk

If you have $10,000 to invest in your options trading and you invest all $10,000 on one trade, you won't stay in the market long if you take a loss on the first trade—that is, if the full $10,000 is at risk. And even if you diversify the risk, and spread the $10,000 across five different options trades, if your total starting capital of $10,000 is still at risk, potentially you could lose the total amount quite quickly. If, on the other hand, you only put a portion of your $10,000 into the market at once, say 20 per cent or $2,000, and then in addition limit the risk on each position to, say, 50 per cent on each trade, you can see immediately that the total amount of money at risk is drastically reduced to $1,000. If you lost on all of those trades, you would still have $9,000 to invest. And that's the principle of limiting your money at risk in the market.

> This is one of the most important aspects of money management. Limiting your total risk in the market at any point in time is essential for allowing you to stay in the market long enough to make those profits. And if you limit this to a consistent percentage, it also reduces your exposure when you are trading poorly and increases it when you are trading well.

For example, if you have limited your total risk to 10 per cent at any point in time, using the above example of a starting bank of $10,000, it would mean a total risk of $1,000 in the market. Let's say you make a profit on your first trades, and your bank is now standing at $15,000. According to your money management rules, you can have 10 per cent of this at risk. This means on your next trades you can risk $1,500 in total. Let's say you make another profit, and this time your bank is standing at $18,000. You can now risk $1,800 in total. But on the next trade, you lose the $1,800. Your total bank is now standing at $16,200 so you can only risk $1,620 in total on the next trades. You can see from this example that by keeping your total amount at risk consistent, you increase exposure when you're doing well, and decrease it when you're not. And this means you'll be able to ride out a lot more losses, until you can start making those profits.

Generally, most traders suggest that you should never risk more than 1 per cent to 5 per cent of your capital on any one trade.

Whether you risk the 1 per cent or the 5 per cent is going to depend on how much starting capital you have. In other words, if you start with $10,000, a 1 per cent risk would only be $100—depending on the volatility of the underlying stock, this might not be enough, as you might find yourself tipped out of the market too quickly. If you risk the 5 per cent, this means you would limit your risk to $500 on any one trade—which might be a bit high, depending on the trade. But if your starting bank is $5,000, the 5 per cent risk might sound right to you. In other words, the percentage you have at risk at any point in time will largely depend on the bank you start with.

 So what does the idea of money at risk actually mean? For example, if you have decided you can risk $500 on one trade, does this mean you cannot undertake any option writing, since this carries unlimited risk? Are you forced to buy options with a total premium of $500? The answer is no. The concept of money at risk means that you have some sort of way of limiting the risk on the trade to $500. In other words, if you write a call with a profile of unlimited risk, you must exit the trade when you have suffered the $500 loss. And if you buy an option for a total premium of $750, it means you must exit the trade when you have suffered the $500 loss—no staying in to see what might happen after that, and no giving away the total premium of $750. The concept of money at risk gives you full flexibility to trade any position, any premium amount, and adopt any loss profile, and at the same time provides a rule for how much loss you can suffer on that one trade.

So how do you limit risk to a predetermined amount?

Limiting Losses—Stop Losses

There are several methods to limit your trading losses. The most commonly recognised method is the use of a **stop loss order**. Basically, a stop loss is an order which sets a predetermined price, which once hit, exits your position 'at market'—that is, at the next traded market price.

Based on money management rules, stop losses set at a predetermined premium amount (based on a set percentage of capital) can be an effective way of limiting risk. So if you have decided that you can risk $500 on a trade and you buy a call option for $1,250, it means you would exit your call when the premium value falls to $750.

Also, as you can see, you are maintaining the rule of increasing exposure and risk when you are trading well and reducing exposure and risk when you are trading poorly.

Now, just because you have set your stop at a certain percentage of the premium doesn't mean you should stay in the market until you have lost this whole amount. Remember, this is a maximum amount at risk on any one trade, it doesn't have to be the actual loss—the stop loss is for worst-case scenario protection. Most traders do not only rely purely on stops based on price—most also look at time and volatility. In other words, your initial analysis should take into account your view on how quickly the market should move, as well as what volatility is expected to do. If you see a sudden adverse move in volatility, or the market doesn't move within the timeframe you expect, you should also think about exiting. In conjunction with your money management stops, this forms a very effective method for limiting loss.

> Now, a word of warning on stop loss orders. Firstly, they do not guarantee the price at which you exit. In other words, since the order is traded at market once your price is hit, it means that the price at which you get filled can be worse than you expect. And even more frustrating, the price can be better, because the market might recover once your stop price has been briefly hit.
> In addition, unfortunately, you cannot place stop loss orders on the Exchange. This doesn't mean you cannot limit your losses, it just means you will have to use a 'mental stop'—that is, monitor your position, and place your order at market when your price is hit. Just beware—it's very tempting to change your mind when using a mental stop. It will take a disciplined mind to follow your money management rules at all times.

Money management stops are especially effective when used for bought positions. They can still be used for sold positions, but you must also remember the other risk—exercise—when you sell. Remember, exercise can be costly—if you wait for your money management rules to take you out of your sold position, you just might find that you're exercised against before they kick in. However, there is another way you can protect yourself against the unlimited risk of writing, and that's through buying protection.

Limiting Losses—Buying Protection

You already know that the writer of a naked call faces potentially unlimited losses as the share price climbs higher and higher above his or her breakeven. In addition, the size of the actual loss will be determined by either the closing price of the call (if the writer exits the position), or through exercise (if the writer is exercised against, and is forced to pay the market price for the shares at that point). The good news is, both of these potential losses can be predetermined through buying protection.

Buying protection for a naked written call simply means that you buy another call at a strike higher than the one written. Since the bought call is further away from the money, the cost will be less than the written position, so the whole transaction should result in a net credit for you (see Figure 14.1, below).

Figure 14.1
Limiting Loss—Buying Protection for Written Call

So how does this actually provide protection? The worst-case scenario for the call writer is a strongly rising market. If the market should start to rise above your written exercise price, it means you will start taking a loss on that position. However, should the market rise above your bought call position, it means your bought call will start to make a profit. This profit will offset any losses as the share price continues to climb. Because of this, you effectively cap the loss potential at this point—that is, the potential loss will be the difference between the two exercise prices, less the net premium received at the start. You could effectively hold both positions as the market continues climbing, safely knowing that you have capped your loss potential.

Of course, there is a second risk to the writer: exercise. You know that once your written call exercise price is breached, your risk of exercise continues to climb with the share price. Should you be exercised against, your obligation will be to deliver shares that you don't already own. However, rather than having to pay the current market price in order to buy your shares (as naked writers do), and having no control over what that price might be, you already know the price you'll pay—you can exercise your bought call, which has given you a predetermined buying price for the shares you must deliver.

The buying of protection in this way turns your initial trade into what's called a 'spread'. For the call writer who buys protection, the spread is referred to as a bear call spread, indicating that profits are made in a bearish market scenario. For the put writer who buys protection, the spread is referred to as a bull put spread, indicating that profits are made in a bullish market scenario.

So you can see how buying protection for your written call position predetermines the maximum loss, and therefore, reduces your risk in the market. But what's the other side of risk reduction? Profit reduction. Protection does not come cheap. In other words, should the share price stay flat or fall, as predicted, and you maximise your profit potential by keeping the whole net premium, because you had to pay for the bought call your return will be lower than had you simply written the call.

Buying protection for a written put position works in a similar way. In other words, you would buy a put at a lower exercise price than the one written (see Figure 14.2, below). In this way, should the worst-case scenario unfold, as the share price falls further and further below your bought put exercise price, your loss is capped at the difference between the two exercise prices, less the net premium received for the overall position. Again, should you be exercised against and have to buy the shares, you could exercise your bought put in order to sell them at a predetermined price. In this way, your potential loss is capped at the start of the trade—and of course, so is your potential profit, which is reduced by the cost of protection.

Figure 14.2
Limiting Loss—Buying Protection for Written Put

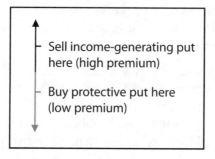

So, the buying of protection for written positions can reduce your risk in the market. In addition, the good news is your margin obligations are also reduced—that is, since your overall risk is less than if you had written a call or put in isolation, your margin requirements to cover that risk are also reduced. (For more information, refer to 'Additional Quick Margining Facts' in Chapter 12.)

Using stop losses and buying protection for your positions are essential elements of any risk management strategy, since they can be effective ways of limiting risk for your trades. But what sort of risk management rules do you need to protect your profits?

Taking Profits—Stop Losses

There are several different ways you can take a profit out of the market. Of course the most basic way is to exit your position, take the money and run. But how do you make sure you don't take profits too soon? How do you 'let your profits run'? Alternatively, how do you make sure you don't leave a profit in the market because you have stayed in too long waiting for that extra return? One of the worst things you can do is give back an already made profit while waiting for an extra gain. So how do you protect your profits against adverse movements, while still allowing you enough time to make that bigger profit?

The use of stop losses is just as important with profits as it is with losses. One of the most effective stops for protecting profits is the trailing stop. The trailing stop is basically a stop which is continually moved as profits are made, so that if the market adversely changes direction and the position is stopped out in the future, it will be for the highest possible profit.

For example, let's say you have bought a put option for 35¢, the market falls, and your put is now worth 63¢. You might place your first stop at 35¢ to protect your initial capital investment—in other words, should the market reverse from where it is and your put fall in value to 35¢, the stop would be triggered, exiting you from the market with close to your initial capital. Let's say that the market continues to fall, and your put is now worth 94¢. You might raise your stop to 63¢, which would mean exiting somewhere around 63¢ if the market should reverse and rise from here. As the market continues to fall and the put increases in value, you would keep raising the value of the stop. In this way, your stop trails the market, protecting your initial capital as well as any new profits made. If the market reverses unexpectedly and your put falls in value to your stop price, you might then be stopped out—but at a predetermined protected profit.

Or on the other hand, let's say you have written a call option for 37¢. The market falls, and the call is now worth 23¢. You might place a stop at 37¢. If the market falls again, and the call premium falls to 12¢, you might place a stop at 23¢. As the market continues to fall and the call continues losing value, you would keep lowering the value of the trailing stop to protect any profits made.

These examples are only to show how the trailing stop works—in other words, they do not attempt to show you where you should actually place the stop. So where should you set the stop for your trade? Obviously, the closer the stop is set to the current premium value, the greater the protection is, but the more likely you could get stopped out during normal daily price fluctuations. On the other hand, the further it is away from the current price, the more profit you will give away if the price moves against you. It can be really tricky setting a stop based on premium alone, since there are so many factors that impact on it and potentially change its value during the day's trading. In other words, if you set a stop based on a premium amount alone, you run the risk of getting stopped out because of thinning market demand or a momentary change in volatility measures. Okay, so it's still at a profit. But this can be frustrating if your stop price is hit, you get tipped out of your trade, and then the market continues moving in your favour.

> One of the most effective ways of setting a profit stop is based on the underlying share price—that is, the stop is placed so that you exit when a particular share price is breached. In this way, you catch any major change in the trend before it does too much damage to your option's profits. The only downside is, you have no control over what the value of the option will be at the time you exit the position.

For example, if you have bought a call, you might look for a share price breach which indicates that the upward trend has now reversed and the price is likely to keep falling. Once you see the share price fall below a predetermined level, you would exit your call at market. If the share price is not breached and continues to rise, you would then look for the next likely point which would indicate a reversal in trend, and place your stop there. As the market is rising, that share price would be higher than the previous stop point, thereby protecting more of your call's profit as the market continues to rise. If you continue this, you can trail the rising market, protecting your profit and at the same time allowing your profits to run.

The use of technical indicators can be really effective for choosing turning points in the market (more on this later). Alternatively, you might place the stop just outside the average daily trading range for the underlying stock—in this way, you eliminate the fear of being stopped out because of normal intra-day fluctuations.

Taking Profits—Rolling, Rolling, Rolling

Stops aren't the only way to take profits out of the market. Another thing you can do is roll your position.

 Rolling basically means closing your existing position, and then immediately taking another position with the same market view—but at a later expiry month or a different exercise price.

For example, let's say you have bought an ABC JUN 400 call for 50¢. Over the next few weeks, the market rises strongly to $5.00, and your call is now worth $1.05. You still have four weeks left on the call option, and think there still could be more upside. But if you wait, the market could start taking profits, and you might find your call losing value on this short-term correction. Instead of placing a trailing stop which will knock you out of the market altogether, you decide to close your JUN 400 call, and then roll forward (that is, to a later expiry) and up (that is, to a higher exercise price). You buy the JUL 500 call which is at-the-money and trading at 50¢, compared to your deep in-the-money JUN which is trading at $1.05. You pocket 55¢ from the transaction, and at the same time, are still in the market to take advantage of any more upside. In the meantime, because you have taken more than your initial capital from the first trade, you effectively have a 'free trade' in the market.

Another example might be where you have bought the ABC JUN 400 call for 50¢, and the market rises strongly and quickly to $5.00. Your 400 call is now worth $1.20, and you still have two more months left before expiry. You think there is more upside—but what if you're wrong? You don't want to lose any upside potential that is still there, but at the same time, you don't want to give huge profits back to the market if you're wrong. This might be a good time to roll up. So you close your JUN 400 call for $1.20 and at the same time buy the JUN 500 call for 55¢. You pocket 65¢ from the transaction, effectively taking some profit from the market, yet are still in the market if there is more upside.

Rolling can be an effective way of removing some profit from the market. Just remember, the new trade needs the same care and attention in regard to loss and profit protection. Don't just leave it on its own because you have initiated a 'free' or low-risk trade—you still have capital at risk. Never forget that.

Taking Profits—Writing Income

 If you have bought an option, there is a third way to protect profits. And that's through the writing of another option in order to remove some income from the market.

For example, let's say you have a bought call option which holds a lot of profit. By writing another call option with a higher exercise price, you earn the premium as income, and effectively pull money out of the market (see Figure 14.3, below). Since your written call has a higher exercise price than the bought one, the premium will be lower, however, if volatility or demand has increased since buying the first call, you might find over-pricing provides an inflated selling price for the second call. And remember delta? Should the share price continue to rise, but no higher than the exercise price of the written call, your bought call will gain in value at a faster rate than the written call. This means that your overall position is still gaining value. And if by expiry the share price is at or below the exercise price of the written call, the written call expires worthless, allowing you to keep all the premium income. In addition, your bought call has also retained its full value.

Figure 14.3
Protecting Profit—Writing Income for Bought Call

Of course, the share price could continue to rise above the written exercise price, and once this happens, you cap any potential profit above this price. That is, the written call will begin to lose value at the same rate as the bought call, thereby eliminating any further profits. In this way, you limit the profit potential to the difference between the two exercise prices, less the overall cost of the trade. And there is another risk—exercise. However, should you be exercised against, you can always exercise your bought call in order to buy the shares at a predetermined price (and profit). So generally, for you to initiate this strategy, your view would be for the share price to rise no further than the higher call exercise price.

But the good news is, if you reduce your profit potential, you also reduce your risk. In other words, should the share price fall below your bought exercise price, and both options expire worthless, rather than losing the full value of the bought call, your loss is reduced by the receipt of income from the written position. So again, this strategy, referred to as a bull call spread, has allowed you to reduce your risk of holding a single bought call within a portfolio. In addition, because of the limited loss potential on the overall position (that is, limited to the total cost of the spread), there are no margin requirements.

A similar strategy can be employed for a bought put position, by writing a put option at a lower exercise price than the bought put (see Figure 14.4, below).

Figure 14.4
Protecting Profit—Writing Income for Bought Put

Buy speculative put here initially (high strike)

Sell income-generating put here later (low strike)

Again, the income produced by writing the second put reduces your overall risk in the market should the share price rise, and so this has to mean that your overall profit potential is also reduced—to the difference between the two exercise prices less the cost of the overall transaction, as the share price continues to fall below the exercise price of the second put. So generally, for you to initiate this strategy, which is referred to as a bear put spread, your view would be for the share price to fall no further than the lower exercise price put—otherwise, you cap your profit potential unnecessarily.

You can see that turning a single bought position into a spread gives you the ability to reduce your overall risk, and at the same time, the profit potential of the trade. So always remember that options are flexible—they allow you to specifically tailor the amount of risk you want to adopt for your share trading.

The Four Most Dangerous Trading Habits

Of course, risk management is as much about what you don't do as it is about what you do. Here are some of the most common mistakes traders make.

1. Rolling losses

Remember how you can roll positions to protect profits in the market? One of the most dangerous things you can do is roll a position that is showing a loss.

 Rolling losses can be a way to avoid the fact that you're taking a loss. But even worse than that, it is a sure way to dramatically increase your exposure to, and your risk of, a losing position.

One of the classic cases of bad trading I've seen over and over again is the rolling of written calls. For example, let's say you enter the market by selling a naked call for 38¢. The market steadily rises over the next few weeks, and your call is now worth 69¢. Not having any risk or money management rules in place, and not wanting to accept the loss by exiting your call, you decide to roll your position by closing and then selling at a higher strike price. After all, the income you earn will offset your loss, and you're pretty sure that the market will exhaust itself soon anyway. You decide to sell an out-of-the-money call to give you a buffer against any further short-term upside potential. The only trouble is, in order for you to make up for the previous loss, you now have to sell two or three out-of-the-money calls. So you are increasing your exposure, your risk and your risk of exercise—all this, and in a rising market.

Now it's not to say that rolling losses this way can't work. It's just that you have to be aware of the high risk that you are adopting. Make sure you aren't rolling a loss because your ego can't bear to crystallise it.

2. Averaging down

This is another classic way of increasing the exposure and risk of a losing position.

> Basically, averaging is a way of entering the market slowly, starting with a small number of contracts and then gradually adding to the position as the market moves. The fact that you have bought several contracts for differing amounts means that the price of each contract is averaged over all the prices.
>
> The rule of good trading says that you only ever average up—that is, you add contracts to your position when the market is moving in your favour. In this way, you don't expose yourself to the risk of a large position until you see the market moving as expected. And while the average price of all the contracts might be higher than if you had bought all the contracts upfront, the risk of buying a large position that might move against you is reduced. You only add to the position on confirmation of your expectations.

For example, rather than buy 10 call options for 27¢ each immediately, you might buy only two to start with and wait to see what the market does before adding to the position. As the market rises, and you feel confident it will continue to go up, you might add two more, and so on. So when you have purchased your 10 contracts, two at a low price, two more at a slightly higher price, and so on, the price of the 10 is averaged out across the full position. This can be an effective way of increasing exposure as a market moves in your favour. Now, contrast this with averaging down.

> Averaging down is still a process of adding to the position as the market moves; however, it is done while the market is moving against you. The trader who averages down is attempting to reduce the average cost of the losing position. Nevertheless, while the average cost is lowered, the total exposure and risk is increased at the same time, and all while the market is moving in the wrong direction.

Let's look at an example of averaging down. Let's say, using the above example, that you still buy the initial two options for 27¢, but that after doing so the market falls. Your premiums are now worth only 20¢. Rather than employ a risk management strategy, you decide to buy two more for 20¢ each, knowing that this reduces the average cost of each position to 23.5¢. The market falls again, and your options are now worth 15¢ each. You buy two more, knowing that this lowers your average price even further, to 21¢ per option. Sound good? Well hopefully, no! Because while your average price per option is falling, you now have six options which will lose value if the market doesn't turn around—a total risk of $1,260, rather than the initial $540. And remember, those first two options you bought for 27¢ are pretty far away from their initial buying price. You need a really good rise in the market for them to recover from time decay and the effect of any further price falls. So, by averaging down, you have greatly increased your exposure in a falling market. And what has it done to your profit potential? If you're buying calls in a falling market, probably not a lot. It's not a very smart practice!

3. Increasing risk to recover from previous losses

The rule of good trading says that you should increase risk when you are trading well, and decrease it when you are trading poorly.

Unfortunately, the market is filled with traders who do the exact opposite. Many are 'revenge trading', desperately trying to return a profit to make up for previous losses—and generally the way they do it is to increase their exposure.

It's a bizarre thing, but lack of confidence often leads to losses. If you have taken a few losses it may be much better to stay on the sidelines, wait until you're more confident, and only increase risk when you have been trading well. And if you have a good money and risk management plan in place, its rules should automatically do this for you.

4. Closing positions to pay for margins owed on new trades

This is another example of bad trading that I have seen over and over again. Traders who do not understand margining requirements run the risk of overtrading. And eventually, that overtrading is going to show as a margin which they cannot afford to pay. The only way to pay it might be to close other existing positions—and these might be the exact positions that have the potential to make huge returns.

Remember, the margining system is in place as a way to assess and manage risk. There's no point in reinventing the wheel. The best guidelines for your own money and risk management are the rules put in place by the Exchange. If the Exchange rule says that you cannot place another trade because you cannot afford the margining requirements, don't do the trade. And only close out a position because your risk management rules tell you to—not because you want to chop and change into another trade. It's wise to get to know and understand how the margining system works, and don't overtrade. And beware juggling positions in order to pay margins; it's a sure way to make a lot of successive losses when you may not need to.

The 10 Rules of Successful Traders

Okay, so by now you've read a lot about money and risk management, and also about what can go horribly wrong. So now it's time to look at what the professional market uses as its golden rules for success:

1. Don't risk significant amounts before key reports, such as balance of payments, CPI, etc., are released.
2. Always use a proactive stop or trend-following system to signal when to get out.
3. Think through all the 'what ifs'. Anticipate and plan, rather than react.
4. If you see you are losing money a lot faster than you've made it, it should be a warning to you.
5. Keeping the risk small and consistent is crucial.
6. If you lose a predetermined amount of your starting capital (10 per cent to 20 per cent), take a breather, try to analyse what went wrong, and wait until you are confident before you start trading again.
7. Patience is a virtue. Learn to wait for confirmation of trades before entering the market. And learn when to stay out.
8. Learn to be disloyal. Never have loyalty to a position, or you'll ignore the signs that tell you it is time to exit.
9. Money is not important. Trading well is important.
10. Never listen to anyone else's advice.

Technical Tools as Perceptual Filters

 One of the key characteristics seen in successful traders is the ability to form trading strategies based on unbiased, unemotional decisions and, in addition, to form a consistent trading strategy that will perform over time.

If markets are continually changing, how can you make sure that your trading is consistent and following the same market indicators that have been successful in the past? And with all the information available in the market, how can you ensure that you form an unbiased view?

Most traders talk about the need for a **perceptual filter** that allows them to focus on relevant market information and, at the same time, provides a disciplined and consistent approach to their trading. So a perceptual filter is a methodology, an approach or a particular system which is automatic, congruent with your way of thinking and making decisions, and which includes specific risk management plans. If used consistently, it provides an effective way of managing your emotional state and of observing the market from the perspective of having no position when you have one. In other words, it provides objectivity in your trading.

Most traders use technical analysis as a perceptual filter for viewing market information. The use of one or more indicators can greatly increase your chances of seeing the valuable market information, discounting the invaluable indicators and forming a consistent strategy that can be tracked over time. So if you find that a particular indicator works for you, you can use it again, with, hopefully, the same results.

Technical analysis is also a means of designing and implementing your money and risk management strategy, providing a way to determine the balance between buying and selling pressure in the market, the trend and whether it's about to reverse or not, specific entry and exit points for a trade, and profit and loss estimates.

It's not going to tell you where the market is going, but it will give you a high probability of where it might go next. If you're right, it will help you maximise your gains. If you're wrong, it will help you minimise your losses. Not only that, it will help remove the emotional knee-jerk reactions to changes in market information.

So what is technical analysis, and how do you use it in your trading?

Using Technical Tools

Technical analysis is the study of the historical price movement of a stock, in order to gain an insight into future or potential market action or price trends. It basically looks at price as a psychological event—that is, as a snapshot of the balance between buyers and sellers in the market at any point of time—and how that psychology changes over time.

And so, the underlying philosophy behind technical analysis is that:

- history repeats itself, so if you follow what the market has done historically and, therefore, know what it is likely to do next, you have a high probability of making a profit when it repeats

- crowds are led by price and if you understand the underlying buying and selling pressure you have a good chance of seeing where the market will go next
- prices move in trends and if you can spot the trend, you can trade with it
- market action discounts the fundamentals of a stock, so it is not necessary to understand what the fundamentals are. You can see their effect by the action in the marketplace—that is, the market psychology.

The whole process of technical analysis is based on four fundamental processes:

1. identify the trend
2. trade the trend
3. identify the end of the trend
4. exit or reverse the trade.

So technical analysis uses price information and overlays various tools in order to:

- establish trends
- predict changes in trend
- find areas of support and resistance to price movements
- predict the intensity of a trend
- predict how long a trend is likely to continue
- show potential buying and selling opportunities
- indicate whether a market is overbought or oversold
- establish timing for price movements.

Most commonly, traders use bar charts showing the open, high, low and close for the day's trading, as well as volume and open interest. They then use a variety of different analytical tools to help predict market movement from these initial indicators of market activity. These tools can be as simple as using trendlines, support and resistance levels or moving averages, or as complex as combining different tools and indicators (such as combining moving averages with a relative strength index) to form trader-specific signals.

Whatever the tool or indicator used, technical analysis provides a perceptual filter that gives discipline, consistency in trading method, a way to determine profit and loss, and a way to uphold money and risk management strategies. And all with a snapshot of the underlying market psychology.

Just beware. There is no Holy Grail of trading, and the use of technical analysis is not going to automatically make you a better trader—technical analysis is an art, not a science. There are many indicators and tools, many ways of using them, many interpretations of signals, and many ways of acting on the information that you see. So how do you decide which indicators to use for your trading?

I See Dead People

Okay, so we all felt a little creepy when the little boy in the movie, *The Sixth Sense*, claimed he could see dead people. Especially since no-one else in the movie could see them. Clearly, out of all the information in the environment, he was able to see something more than everyone else could, and he acted on that information. Were the ghosts 'real' because he could see them? They were to him, even if everyone else had a hard time believing it. And that's what can happen when you start looking at charts. Chart information can be open to interpretation. What you see and what you act on may be quite different to what everyone else is seeing—after all, if it weren't the case, there wouldn't be anyone on the other side with whom you could trade. Looking at chart information is a little like looking at clouds—you see a rabbit, I see a castle, someone else sees their mother-in-law in the many shapes that form in the sky. And just because you see something or don't see something, doesn't make it real or not real. So you have to make sure that whatever you're seeing is helping you to trade more effectively.

One of the easiest ways to start looking at technical analysis is through the many different charting patterns—tops and bottoms, head and shoulders, rising wedges, and flags form just a few of the many different types of patterns which claim to be predictive indicators. Most people start off their charting careers by looking at the selection of these patterns and what they mean to potential price movement.

 But a word of warning on chart patterns. Generally, these types of indicators won't be enough to make you a long-term successful trader.

That's largely because of the level of interpretation needed to see these patterns. And even if you do see them forming, whether they complete or not is another thing. Often, chart patterns are most successfully seen in retrospect—not very helpful for your trading! So most successful traders use other indicators besides chart patterns for their trading—moving averages, stochastics and relative strength indicators are just a few of the more common types used.

 Whatever indicator or set of indicators you use, make sure that it suits your temperament, style of trading and depth of pocket. It's no good having a signal to enter the market if you can't or won't follow it.

For example, if the signal you choose has you in and out many times during the day and your philosophy is for longer-term holding strategies, more than likely you won't follow the signal anyway. And unless you have live data to follow during the day, you won't know the signal has generated an entry for you anyway. In addition, if the stops it selects are too rich for your money management, there's not much point using them. Better to find another type of indicator that will more closely follow your own personal style of trading and making decisions. Remember, the whole idea of following a particular indicator is so it makes your trading easier, less emotional and more automatic.

 Any technical strategy you employ should also be tested over a period of time.

For example, if your signal is that you always buy when a 10-day moving average crosses a 30-day moving average, you might find this works with some stocks better than others. Test it over as much historical data as possible, and even better, test it with some hypothetical trades in the current environment. The longer the period you test it over, the more robust, or less robust, it might appear. And you need to know that.

 Most traders use a combination of different analytical tools for their trading. No one indicator is likely to be the answer to your trading—if there were one foolproof indicator, the markets would fail, since everyone would be using the same one. Every tool has advantages and disadvantages—some are best in trending markets, some are better at predicting trend changes from congestion, some are better at predicting changes in timing, some warn of impending tops or bottoms. Find the set of tools that work for you, and stick to them. After all, since the majority of traders lose their money and only a minority make the huge returns, it must mean that the minority have the ability to see something that the rest of us cannot. The most successful traders find new ways of looking at and using market information—and they're unlikely to tell you what that is. So rather than trying to use someone else's set of technical tools, try to find your own.

A good grounding in the range of different tools is invaluable—after all, unless you first understand what they are and how you can use them, you are unlikely to find the ones that will give you that trading edge. A good place to find information on technical analysis is the Australian Technical Analysts Association (or ATAA) at www.ataa.com.au.

A Word on Black Box Trading

Over the years I have had a lot of investors ask me about different black box systems and whether they are likely to be profitable or not. And while there is no 'Holy Grail' answer to this, there are some things which you should take into account before you consider buying one.

Basically, a black box system is one which gives you entry and exit signals, so that you don't have to pick and choose trades yourself. And theoretically, these systems are 'tried and true', often promising extremely high returns—all, usually for a very high price tag. And that's where I get very suspicious. After all, if you had a system that could pick major market trends and return huge profits, would you sell it to other investors?

Beware of trying to find the Holy Grail of trading via one of these systems. It's not that black box systems don't or can't work—I've seen some systems used by the professional market that have been extremely successful. It's just that before you buy one, you want to make sure it's going to work for you. Here are a few suggestions for deciding whether a system will work for you or not:

1. Make sure the system has been tested over a reasonable period of time. This should be at least one year, but the longer the better—this makes it more likely that the trading results are not an anomaly, and are likely to be more robust.
2. Make sure the system was tested using real trades, not just hypothetical trading. Just as it is with paper-trading, the actual entry and exits you get can make a huge difference to the overall results. It's also more comforting to know the owners of the system felt confident enough to invest their own money using its signals.

3. Make sure the system's trading results take brokerage and other transaction fees into account. Transaction fees can make a huge difference to your trading results—especially if the system has you in and out of the market often.

4. Make sure the system works with the amount of money you want to invest. After all, there's no point investing in a system that requires a minimum of $50,000 to get good results if you only have $25,000 to invest.

5. Find out the largest draw-down of the system since it has traded, and make sure it fits your money and risk management rules. The worst possible scenario is that you invest just as the system hits its largest acceptable draw-down—you have to be able to weather it if you are going to continue trading via the system. In other words, if the largest acceptable unrealised or realised loss was $40,000, and you only have $25,000 to invest, the system is not going to work for you.

6. Make sure the system suits your trading style. It's no good if you are a long-term investor, with little time to spend on your trading, if the system has you in and out several times during the day. It really needs to suit your temperament, trading style, needs and objectives.

7. Ask to speak with a few clients who have bought the system, and make sure they have invested a similar amount to you. Ask the clients when they started, how much time and money they have invested, and what results they have seen. If clients are making money from the system, the owners should have no problem selecting a few happy customers with whom you can talk.

8. If you use the system, make sure you follow every trade, as indicated. It's no good if you start to interfere with the trading, choosing particular trades, ignoring others—the whole point of using a black box system is to eliminate the need for picking and choosing. And you will not get the same results if you don't follow it precisely. Another good reason why it has to suit your temperament, risk and money management rules, and size of starting capital.

The cliché in the market is that money and risk management is more important than using a particular trading method. And it's true; but if your trading method isn't based on sound rules of probability, your risk management system isn't going to help you much—except to help you lose your money more slowly. Nevertheless, overall, most successful traders will say that market analysis accounts for only 20 per cent of overall market success—and that means the remaining 80 per cent is accounted for by risk- and self-management. Controlling your emotions, as well as the amount you have at risk at any point in time, are two crucial ways of limiting loss and promoting profit.

A risk and money management strategy allows you to decide:

- how much starting capital you will allocate for trading
- how much money you will have at risk at any point in time
- how you will limit losses
- when you will take profits.

15

THE
BUSINESS
OF TRADING

Chapter objectives:

- Enable you to find a broker
- Define the accreditation requirements of options brokers
- Discuss the costs of trading
- Enable you to open an account with a broker
- Explain client documentation.

I heard a joke once about how the devil came down to visit a very prestigious stockbroking firm. He spoke with all the brokers, listened to their advice, weighed up all their characters and quality of advice, and finally selected one. The devil offered the broker everything in the world he could ever want—fame, fortune, long life, etc. All the broker had to do in return was to surrender his soul, the soul of his family, and the souls of the next five generations beyond that. And the broker's response? "Yeah? What's the catch?"

Okay, so brokers have had a bad rap from some people over the years. But there are good and bad brokers, just the way there are good and bad doctors, lawyers and plumbers. The trick is to find a good one. So how do you find a good broker for your options trading? And what can you expect from him or her once found?

Finding a Broker

Generally, finding a broker is not difficult. The difficulty is in finding a good broker. Not because there are lots of 'bad' brokers out there, but because it depends on what your definition of a 'good' broker is—in other words, you need to know what it is you are looking for in a broker.

The range of services brokers offer start at non-advisory at one end of the scale, to full discretionary trading (that is, your broker can place orders for you without prior approval by you) at the other end—and in between, advisory services. Which you select will depend completely on your needs, style of trading and trading temperament.

A good place to start is always with your current broker, assuming you're happy with the service and relationship that you have for your share trading. You must make sure your broker is accredited to give advice in options if you are looking for an advisory service. (More on this later.) Another way to find a broker is through friends—if your friend is happy with his or her broker, you might find you're able to also build a good working relationship with that person. Alternatively, the Exchange offers a referral service, and also places the names of accredited advisers on its website.

So what makes a good broker? Here are some guidelines for finding one that suits your needs:

- If you require advice, you must make sure your broker is accredited. If you simply need an execution-only style of broker (that is, you plan to do all your own analysis and place orders without any advice from your broker), your broker may not need to be accredited.
- You should feel comfortable with your broker, and have the ability to build a good rapport with him or her. It's the same with any professional relationship. Bear in mind that this person is going to be your lifeline to the market. If you don't feel you communicate well, it doesn't augur well for a successful long-term relationship.
- Your broker should understand your investment style and needs. This goes beyond simply taking down your information in the 'know your client' documentation. There should be an ongoing dialogue between the two of you regarding the types of trades you should employ. And if your broker is constantly

offering trades that don't suit your style, objectives, or money and risk management, find someone who does.

- A good broker talks in plain language, and doesn't try to coerce you into any trade. Beware the broker who tries to bamboozle you with jargon, or who pushes you into a trade that you don't understand or are not comfortable with.

- Your broker should be reasonably easy to access and not too busy to talk with. You need to speak with your broker at least once a day. And beware brokers who are only available via their assistants—after all, you're paying for their advice and service, not their assistants'.

- You need to make sure your broker has direct access to the market via a trading screen. There's not much point placing an order with someone who then has to make a phone call to place your order with someone else.

- Some brokers provide clearing as well as trading services, while some only provide trading services. Just make sure that whoever you go with, you understand the services that are and are not provided. And whatever level of service is provided, you should expect to get your trading documentation promptly and within the time specified by the Exchange.

- The cost of commission does not necessarily guarantee you get what you pay for. More expensive doesn't have to mean better. Make sure you understand the charges your broker passes on to you, and what you get for your money (e.g. access to research, a direct line to your broker as opposed to his or her assistant, trading screen on premises—more on commissions later).

Just a word on online brokers. Online services can be a really quick and efficient way of trading when you don't require any advice from a broker. However, at time of writing there are no online services which include options trading. There are some brokers who offer an email order placement service, but this is only a replacement to placing your order via the phone. It is not what's known as 'straight-through processing', whereby the order is automatically sent to the market (as in the current screen-traded system of the Exchange, or some online order services).

If you want to use an email order service, just be aware that in a fast-moving market, it cannot replace the speed of placing an order directly to your broker via the telephone. Apart from that, you will miss out on any new information that your broker might be aware of before you place the trade. However, if you do intend to trade via email, it is important to make sure that there is someone on the other side dedicated to the screen. Ask your broker if there is a dedicated person, and what the average delay is in getting an order placed on screen. You don't want to find that in an active market your email order is waiting in a long queue, rather than already placed into the market.

Notice how there's nothing on our list that says that a broker should provide good advice? Let's face it, brokers don't know where the market is going any more than you or I do. The most successful traders do their own analysis—and so should you. And if you do your own analysis, the good news is you might find a discount non-advisory broker just as good as a full-service broker. In the meantime, if you are looking for someone to give advice, be aware that options brokers range from those who do a few buy writes every now and then for select clients, right up to 'rocket scientist' options specialists who do nothing but trade options. It's really up to you who you decide to go with. But for my money, I'd much rather know my broker is serious about options trading—and one of the ways you can determine that is via the accreditation process.

On top of commissions paid to your broker, you will also be required to pay certain Exchange fees when you trade. These transaction fees include an Exchange registration fee (at time of writing, $1.12 per contract), as well as an exercise fee (at time of writing, 55¢).

Accredited Advisers

Accreditation was introduced by the Exchange a few years ago, and is a process which aims to set minimum competency standards for brokers advising clients on options trading.

The emphasis on the process is for anyone giving advice to clients—hence, 'no advice' brokers generally fall outside the scope of the program. It doesn't mean they can't provide a really good, discounted execution-only style service—but you won't get any advice from them. On the other hand, just because a broking firm only offers a non-advisory service doesn't mean its brokers aren't accredited—quite a few non-advisory firms have submitted their brokers to the rigours of the accreditation testing anyway.

 The accreditation program offered by the Exchange includes a non-mandatory training program and a mandatory examination for brokers. Brokers must pass the exams at a mastery level of 80 per cent, and in addition, must have the broking firm sign-off on the accreditation before they can call themselves an accredited adviser.

Accreditation is offered on two levels:

- Level One is required for any broker wanting to advise on warrants, buying options, and selling options to close a bought position.
- Level Two is required for any broker wanting to advise on writing options, and on other more complex option strategies.

Whether you choose a Level One or Level Two adviser will depend on the type of trading you are going to do. Just be aware—if you select a Level One adviser now, you won't be able to do anything besides buy options. And more than likely, your needs will change over time. So, it might be better to start with a Level Two adviser straightaway—there are far fewer of them, but at least you know they have gone that extra step and have that extra level of knowledge about the market. And more than likely, if they have gone to the trouble of gaining Level Two accreditation it's because they are more active in the market.

Once you have decided on the type of service and level of accreditation you require, I suggest you ring at least six different brokers to start with. See how accessible they are, how friendly they are, how easily you communicate with each other, and whether they are interested in trading for your size account. I know this sounds like a lot of phone calls, but believe me, out of the six or so you call, I can guarantee you will soon cut the list to two or three whom you want to speak with in person. Once you get that far, ask them about their backgrounds—how long they have traded options, what level of accreditation they have, whether they trade for themselves (although some firms will not allow this, viewing it as a conflict of interests), what type of clients they have, what size accounts they normally look after, their preferred trading strategies, and their preferred methodology. If you can, ask to get referrals from three of their clients—one who has been with them a year, one for six months, and one for three months. If their clients are doing well, they shouldn't mind giving you the references.

The Costs of Trading

Commissions are always one of the most talked about topics amongst new traders. How much are commissions? How are they charged? How much should you pay?

Commissions on options transactions differ from share transactions in that they are completely negotiable between you and your broker.

There are three different ways brokers generally charge commissions:

1. As a flat fee, charged on a per transaction basis. As a rough guide, at the time of writing you will probably expect to pay somewhere around $25 for a non-advisory order placement, and $40 to $50 for an advisory service. Just be aware, this is for each 'leg'—in other words, you will pay that to open, and pay that again to close the transaction.
2. As a percentage of the premium value.
3. As a combination of both flat fee and a percentage of premium value. Generally, this is if the percentage of the premium value is small—the broker then has the flexibility to charge you a flat fee for that particular trade.

Be aware that the more trading you do, the more flexible your broker is going to be on your commissions. The more trading you're going to do, the less your commission rate is likely to be. The same can be said if you open a relatively large dollar value account as opposed to a relatively small dollar value account. Make sure you negotiate this upfront—there's no point telling your broker how active you're going to be after they have charged you full brokerage.

As a general rule, you can usually negotiate a lower commission rate on:

- frequent large trading lots, for example, if you plan to trade 50 lots every time
- buy writes, since the broker is going to charge commission on the share transaction as well
- multi-legged transactions, for example, naked writing with bought protection
- frequent exercise, since there are other Exchange fees involved in exercise.

One of the most constant complaints of traders is the paying of commission to a broker. Woody Allen quips aside, you will never go broke paying commission. You will go broke with poor money and risk management. If you're making money overall with your trading, I can guarantee you will never complain about paying commission, any more than you complain about your mechanic's fees if your car's getting a good service. And the good news on fees is that there is no stamp duty on option transactions, or on the securities transactions that result from options exercise.

Opening an Account

Okay, so now you know what you need from your broker, you know what services your broker offers, you feel comfortable with your rapport and your broker's level of experience and knowledge on the markets, and you have negotiated your commission scale. You're now ready to open your account with your broker.

Before opening the account, the Exchange requires you to:

1. Sign a Client Agreement form with your broker

The Client Agreement sets out all the terms and conditions that cover your relationship with your broker. In addition, it declares that you have read and understood the risk disclosure statement; you have read and understood the Exchange's booklet *Understanding Options Trading*; that the broker will call you for margins; and that you are bound by the Exchange's business rules.

2. Sign a risk disclosure

3. Read the Exchange's booklet Understanding Options Trading

While your broker will supply you with a copy of the Exchange's booklet, it's a good idea to get one beforehand. The Exchange offers the booklet free of charge in hardcopy, but you can also download it free straight from its website.

4. Provide the 'know your client' information to your broker

Hopefully, you already have made a list of the information required using Chapter 14, 'Managing Your Position and Your Money'. Alternatively, there's a great tool on the Exchange's website which allows you to print off the relevant information and take it straight to your broker.

Client Documentation

Once you start trading, you'll need some way to track your positions. Under the Exchange's business rules your broker has to provide you two main documents: contract notes and open position statements.

1. Contract notes

Every time you trade, you must receive a contract note which shows all the details of the trades, including the number of contracts, whether you have bought or sold, the price at which you bought or sold and whether it's an opening or closing transaction.

2. Open position statements

At the end of the month, your broker must send you an open position statement if you have any current positions in the market. This statement details each position, including the current traded price.

Just be aware, if the broker you place your orders with is not a clearing broker, you might find your paperwork is sent from a different, clearing broker. If this is the case, it should be outlined in the Client Agreement you sign.

The Exchange's website has an interactive demonstration of these two documents and the type of information they contain. It's a good idea to acquaint yourself with these before you start trading, and if there's anything you don't understand, ask your broker. And one final word on documentation—keep it! Come taxation time, these statements form an invaluable trail of your trading history.

16 Final Analysis

I heard a great story once, of a woman who wanted to know all the answers to trading, and so moved into a cave in the mountains in order to study with a famous guru. She told the guru that she wanted to know everything there is to know, and begged him to teach her, and so he agreed. He supplied her with stacks of books, a computer with every technical analysis program available, live data for her to follow, and then left her alone so she could study.

Every morning the guru returned to the cave to monitor the woman's progress. In one hand, he carried a heavy wooden cane. And each morning, he asked her the same question: "Have you learned everything there is to know yet?"

Each morning her answer was the same. "No," she said, "I haven't."

The guru would then strike her over the head with his cane and leave her alone again.

This scenario repeated itself for several weeks. Every day the same question, every day the same answer, and every day the same battering. Then one day the guru entered the cave, asked the same question and heard the same answer, only this time when he raised his cane to strike her, the woman grabbed the cane, stopping it in mid-air. The woman was now afraid more than ever. She slowly looked up at the guru, but to her surprise, he was smiling.

"Congratulations," he said, "You have graduated. You now know everything there is to know about trading."

More than a little relieved, but still confused, the woman asked, "How's that?"

The guru replied, smiling, "You have learned that you will never learn everything there is to know, and you have learned to stop the pain."

Okay, by now you've learned a whole lot of information on options—what they are, how they can be used, what strategies you can put in place and why, and how you can manage your position and your money. You've read all the theories, facts, and rules about options—their pricing, how time decay affects premiums, how the professional market prices them, when and how to take profits and losses. You must know all you need to know to make you a successful trader. Or do you?

While a good grounding in theory is essential before you start trading, unfortunately, sometimes the realities of trading fall short of the theories. Sometimes call premiums fall in value when the share price rises (maybe volatility fell). Sometimes if you sell an in-the-money option near expiry you won't recoup the full intrinsic value of the option (after all, if someone pays the full amount to you, how can he/she make any further profit from it?). Sometimes no matter how great your analysis or risk management strategy is, you still make a loss. And no matter how well you think you know yourself, sometimes you won't be as disciplined or unemotional as you'd like to believe. Think of this as the moving feast of options—no matter how much you know, no matter how long you trade, no matter how well you think you know yourself, just as the guru says, there is always more to learn. And that's part of the fun of it. Good luck!

KEY WORDS AND CONCEPTS

Accreditation The Exchange's process which sets minimum competency standards for advisory brokers.

Accredited adviser A broker who has satisfied the Exchange's accreditation requirements. (See also *Level One adviser* and *Level Two adviser*.)

Annualised percentage return Return for the writer, expressed as an annualised percentage which can be used to compare with other potential returns (for example, bank returns) to see exactly what you could be achieving for the year. Generally assumes that the underlying stock is unchanged in price by expiry.

Ask The lowest price that someone is willing to receive for selling an option.

At-the-money call A call option with an exercise price at the current share price.

At-the-money put A put option with an exercise price at the current share price.

Averaging down Systematically adding contracts to an existing losing position and averaging the price per contract across all positions.

Averaging up Systematically adding contracts to an existing profitable position and averaging the price per contract across all positions.

Back-to-back contracts Holding the same number of bought and sold option series within a portfolio. Generally, this is a result of incorrectly closing an existing position—for example, failing to tell the broker that the order to buy is a liquidating order for an existing sold position.

Bid The highest price that someone is willing to pay to buy an option.

Bid/ask spread The difference between the bid and the ask.

Buy write The simultaneous writing of a call and the purchase of the same number of shares underlying the option.

Buying protection (for sold positions) Buying a higher strike call for sold call positions, or buying a lower strike put for sold put positions.

Call option The right to buy.

Call taker Person who has the right to buy the underlying shares.

Call writer Person who assumes the obligation to sell the underlying shares.

Clearing broker A broking firm which clears and settles options contracts on behalf of clients directly with the Exchange's clearing house. The clearing broker settles margins with the clearing house on behalf of all its clients, and sends trading paperwork to clients.

Client Agreement form An agreement which sets out the terms and conditions that cover a trader's relationship with his or her broker. Traders must sign one before trading, acknowledging that they have read and understood the risk disclosure statement and the Exchange's booklet, and agree to abide by the Exchange's business rules.

Close of day price information End of day information such as the day's open, high, low and close, as well as volume and open interest.

Collateral Cash, securities, bank guarantees or other forms of securities used to cover margin requirements.

Collateral offsets Reduction of collateral required for payable margins within an options account where the risk has been reduced or offset by another options position. For example, if the writer of a low strike call buys a higher strike call with the same expiry month and having the same underlying stock, the unlimited risk of the outright written position is reduced, thereby allowing for a collateral offset (that is, margin reduction) for that particular options account.

Combination order Order to fill both sides of the order simultaneously or not at all.

Company option An equity option that has been issued by the underlying company. Exercise of a company option results in an increase in the issued share capital for that particular company.

Contract note Client documentation sent by the broker to the client, outlining all the details of a trade.

Covered call writer Writer of a call who owns the exact number of underlying shares to cover that call.

Delayed prices Market information shown on a delayed time basis, for example, 20 minutes behind the actual market movement.

Delta A measure of how much an option's premium will move when the share price moves.

Delta hedging Using delta to instate the correct level of hedging (that is, full or partial) needed for a share position or portfolio.

Delta rolling Adjusting the delta of the hedging instruments so that the correct level of hedging (that is, full or partial) is maintained within a portfolio.

Derivatives Trading Facility (DTF) Screen-traded system used for options trading.

Discretionary trading Transactions placed on your behalf by your broker, for your trading account, but without reference to you prior to order placement.

Exchange traded option An equity option that has been listed by the Exchange. (Versus *company option*.)

Exercise To take up the right underlying the option.

Exercise price The specified price at which the taker of an option can buy or sell shares.

Expiry cycle Months in which the different option stocks trade. At the time of writing, there are three different expiry cycles in which a stock can trade: January/April/July/October, February/May/August/November, or March/June/September/December.

Fair value The theoretical real value of an option according to a pricing model.

Fill and kill order Order which can be partly filled and the remainder cancelled.

Fill or kill order Order which must be filled entirely or cancelled immediately.

Good for day order Order which remains until the end of day if not filled immediately.

Hedging Taking an equal but opposite position to your physical shareholding.

Implied volatility A measure of expected volatility in the underlying stock based on current market option prices. Expressed as a percentage, implied volatility is a measure of how far the share price is likely to move up or down over a specific period of time.

In-the-money call A call option with an exercise price lower than the current share price.

In-the-money put A put option with an exercise price higher than the current share price.

Intra-day margin A margin which is called, and must be paid, during the trading day instead of the following day.

Intrinsic value The advantage through exercise of your option. For a call option, it is when the exercise price is lower than the current share price. For a put option, it is when the exercise price is higher than the current share price.

Know-your-client rule Corporations Law rules that your broker must make a list of your needs, goals and risk-carrying ability prior to making a trading recommendation to you.

Level One adviser A broker accredited to advise on warrants, buying options, and selling options to close.

Level Two adviser A broker accredited to advise on writing options and on more complex option strategies.

Limit order Order to buy (or sell) at a specified price or better.

Live data A live feed into market prices, volatility, volume, etc., which shows market movement as it happens.

Margin interval An historical volatility measure calculated by the Exchange which shows how far the share price is likely to move up or down from its current price.

Margining A process which calls upon option writers to pay losses every day as they make them.

Market makers Professional traders with trading and quote request obligations.

Market order Order to buy (or sell) at the best price immediately.

Money at risk The total percentage of trading capital that is at risk from current trading positions.

Naked call writer Writer of a call who does not have underlying share ownership.

Non-advisory broker A broker who will take and place orders on your behalf, but cannot offer advice.

Novation A process whereby the Exchange breaks the link between option buyers and sellers, and acts as middleman between the two parties. In this way, neither party has to seek the original party on the other side in order to exit the position.

Open interest Number of buyers and sellers who are holding open positions.

Open position statement Client documentation sent by the broker each month, detailing any open positions held by the client at the end of that month.

Options Clearing House (OCH) The Exchange's clearing house for options.

Out-of-the-money call A call option with an exercise price higher than the current share price.

Out-of-the-money put A put option with an exercise price lower than the current share price.

Perceptual filter A methodology, an approach or a particular system which is automatic, congruent with your way of thinking and making decisions, and which includes specific risk management plans. If used consistently, it provides an effective way of managing your emotional state and providing trading objectivity.

Premium The option's cost. Total premium = intrinsic value + time value.

Premium margin A margin amount required to be paid by the writer of an option, representing the option's market value at close of business the previous day. The premium margin is one half of the total margin requirements. (See *risk margin*.)

Profit and loss profile Also called a payoff diagram or expiry diagram. A graph which shows whether a particular option trade will make a profit or loss (not including commissions and other costs of trading) according to where the share price is at expiry.

Put option The right to sell.

Put taker Person who has the right to sell the underlying shares.

Put writer Person who assumes the responsibility to buy the underlying shares.

Quote request Request for a market maker to provide a bid/ask quote.

Risk margin A margin amount required to be paid by the writer of an option, representing the option's theoretical value should the share price move to the worst-case scenario. The risk margin is one half of the total margin requirements. (See *premium margin*.)

Risk-carrying ability A gauge that tells you how able you are to recover from losses and therefore how risky your investments can be.

Rolling Closing an existing position, and then immediately taking another position with the same market view—but at a later expiry month or a different strike.

Rolling down Closing an existing position, and then immediately taking another position with the same market view, but at a lower exercise price.

Rolling forward Closing an existing position, and then immediately taking another position with the same market view, but at a later expiry month.

Rolling up Closing an existing position, and then immediately taking another position with the same market view, but at a higher exercise price.

Sold strangle The simultaneous sale of an out-of-the-money call and an out-of-the-money put, both with the same expiry date and same underlying stock.

Spot month The current month.

Stop loss order An order which sets a predetermined price, which once hit, exits your position at the next traded market price.

Straight-through processing The order is automatically sent to the market (as in the current screen-traded system of the Exchange).

Strike price See *exercise price*.

Synthetic position A strategy involving two or more instruments which have the same risk/reward profile as another strategy. In other words, you acquire the same exposure for the same risk using multiple instruments as you would have using one.

Synthetic written put A buy write.

Technical analysis The study of the historical price movement of a stock, in order to gain an insight into future or potential market action or price trends.

TIMS (Theoretical Intermarket Margining System) The Exchange's margining system.

Total margin requirement Premium margin + risk margin.

Volatility Size and frequency of share price movements.

Zero-sum game The concept that opposite sides of the same transaction have the exact opposite risk/reward.

INDEX

spot months 66
spread width 128–129
standardisation 11
Stock Exchange Automated
 Trading System (SEATS) 129
stop losses 165–166
strike price 12–13, 146–147

technical analysis 174, 175
—analysis software 144
—information 142–143
—tools 173–174
Theoretical Intermarket Margining
 System (TIMS) 133, 136, 140
theoretical value 135
time 19, 21, 36, 65–66
—decay 20, 42, 43, 66, 89
—premium 66
—value 87–88
traders, professional 63, 125–126
trading
—costs 185–186
—personality 79
—range 118–119
—tools 144

trailing stops 166
trendlines 175

Understanding Options Trading
 187

volatility 21–22, 40, 60, 61, 89,
 90, 118
—historical 59–60, 149
—implied 25, 149, 150
volume 148

websites 144, 151
written strangle pricing factors
 122

zero-sum game 51, 52, 58, 104,
 105